HUSTLER's DIRTIEST Jokes

HUSTLER's DIRTIEST Jokes

Edited by

LARRY FLYNT

CITADEL PRESS
Kensington Publishing Corp.
www.kensingtonbooks.com

CITADEL PRESS BOOKS are published by

Kensington Publishing Corp.
850 Third Avenue
New York, NY 10022

All Kensington titles, imprints, and distributed lines are available at special quantity discounts for bulk purchases for sales promotions, premiums, fund-raising, educational, or institutional use. Special book excerpts or customized printings can also be created to fit specific needs. For details, write or phone the office of the Kensington special sales manager: Kensington Publishing Corp., 850 Third Avenue, New York, NY 10022, attn: Special Sales Department; phone 1-800-221-2647.

CITADEL PRESS and the Citadel logo are Reg. U.S. Pat. & TM Off.

First printing: February 2006

10   9   8   7   6   5   4   3

Printed in the United States of America

Library of Congress Control Number: 2005928268

ISBN 0-8065-2732-3

HUSTLER's DIRTIEST Jokes

1

While cashing his paycheck at the liquor store, John was approached by a woman soliciting donations for charity. "Excuse me, sir, but I represent the Feed the Africans Foundation," the charity worker began. "Before you throw away all your money, I thought you might want to know that for $10 a month, you can feed an entire family in Africa. Will you just think about that, sir?"

John walked out a changed man. Instead of blowing his money inside the liquor store like he normally did, he headed straight for a travel agency and bought his wife and three children a set of one-way tickets to Africa.

2

Q: What did one tampon say to the other?
A: Nothing. They were both stuck up bitches.

3

A biker couple was strolling down Main Street, gazing in the shop windows. Passing a jewelry store, the girlfriend spotted a pretty turquoise skull ring. "Shit!" she exclaimed. "I'd love to have that."

"No problem, honey," her old man replied. He threw a brick through the window and grabbed the ring.

Passing a clothing store, his girlfriend gazed at a leather jacket. "That's so fine!"

He smashed the window with a brick and hauled the jacket out.

"Oh, man!" exclaimed the girlfriend outside a shoe store. "I've gotta have those boots."

"Shit, baby," groused her old man. "Do you think I'm made of bricks?"

4

A rich old man went to the doctor with his young wife. "Let's see," said the doctor, "I need a urine specimen, a stool and a sperm sample."

"Eh? What'd he say?" the old man asked, turning to his wife.

"He said he needs a pair of your underwear."

5

A big slob with prison tattoos walked into a bank and approached a teller. "I'd like to open a fucking checking account," he announced.

"Excuse me, sir?" the teller huffed.

"I want to open a fucking checking account."

"Sir," came the nasal reply, "that kind of language is inappropriate. You'll have to speak to our manager."

As the manager approached, the slob caught his eye. "Hey, man, I just won $20 million in the lottery, and I want to open a fucking checking account."

The manager greeted him with a broad grin. "And this cunt won't help you?"

6

The HUSTLER Dictionary defines *alimony* as: the price of freedom.

7

Coming back from the ladies' room, the bimbo stormed up to her boyfriend at the bar. "That man by the pool table just insulted me!" she fumed. "He told me he wanted to tear my shirt off and suck my tits."

"Yeah?" Her boyfriend jumped from his stool.

"Then he said he was going to rip off my skirt and kiss my pussy!"

"I'm gonna kick his ass!" Her boyfriend pulled his jacket off.

"You better!" the girlfriend egged him on. "Because then he said he was going to turn me on my head, fill my cunt with whiskey and drink it all down!"

Her boyfriend sheepishly took his jacket back and resumed sitting on the bar stool.

"What's wrong?" his girlfriend whined.

"I'm not going to mess with any guy who can drink
that much whiskey."

8

Q: What does a blonde wear behind her ears to attract
   men?
A: Her ankles.

9

Jim's boss accosted him for the third time that week.
"Do you see that, Jim?! All the other guys are carrying
two buckets of cement, and you're just carrying one.
What do you think that means?"

"Looks like you ought to yell at those guys for being
too goddamn lazy to make two trips."

10

Sick and tired of their history professor's lewd jokes
and sexual innuendo, a group of girls decided that the
next time he uttered an inappropriate remark they
would get up and leave in protest. However, overhear-

ing their plan and looking to score some points with the teacher, a fellow student informed him of their scheme.

The next day, after chatting about current events for a few minutes, the teacher suddenly smiled and, making a clever segue, said, "You know, I hear there's a shortage of whores in Paris . . ."

Exchanging resolute looks, the girls rose as one and started to leave the room. Following them with innocent eyes, the professor said, "Girls, where are you going? The next plane doesn't leave till tonight."

11

Q: Why should priests be allowed to marry?
A: So they'll have a better idea of what Hell is really like.

12

The HUSTLER Dictionary defines *condom* as: a child-proof container.

13

This fellow had been assured by his fiancee that she was a virgin. Given the state of modern morals, however, he didn't completely trust her, so he devised a little quiz for their wedding night. Pulling down his pajamas, he asked, "Honey, can you tell me what this is?"

"A wee-wee," she answered coyly.

Delighted by her naiveté, the new husband corrected her gently, "No, sweetheart, it's a prick."

"Uh-uh. It's a wee-wee," insisted his bride, shaking her head. Slightly annoyed, he took her to task. "It's time for you to learn a few things, dear. Now, this is a prick."

"No way," she retorted. "It's not half as big as some of the pricks I've seen!"

14

At a party, the hostess served a politician a cup of punch and told him it was spiked. Next, she served some to a minister. "I would rather commit adultery than allow liquor to pass my lips," he proclaimed.

Overhearing this, the politician poured his punch back and said, "I didn't know we had a choice."

15

While staggering down the main street of town, a drunk somehow managed to make it up a flight of stairs into the cathedral. There he crashed from pew to pew, eventually working his way to a side aisle and into a confessional booth. A priest had been observing the man's sorry progress and, figuring the fellow was in need of some assistance, entered his own side of the confessional. But the priest's attention was rewarded only by a lengthy silence. Finally, he asked, "May I help you, my son?"

"I dunno," came the drunk's voice from behind the partition. "Got any paper on your side?"

16

A fellow had gone to his doctor for a routine checkup, and when the physician entered the examination room, he said gravely, "Harry, I think you'd better sit down. I've got some good news and some bad news."

"Okay, Doc," said Harry, "give me the bad news first."

"Well," said the doctor, "you've got terminal cancer. It's spreading at an unbelievably rapid rate, it's totally inoperable, and you've only got three weeks to live."

"Geez," said Harry, wiping a bead of sweat off his brow. "What's the good news?"

"You know that really cute receptionist out front?"

"You bet!" said Harry.

"The one with the big tits and the sweet little ass?"

"Right!"

"Well," said the doctor, leaning forward with a smile, "I'm fucking her!"

17

At home a gay couple who had spent many years to-gether were relaxing with some wine when one of them declared wistfully, "Our life has been so happy, but still I feel incomplete. If only we could have a child, I would be truly happy." His partner suggested that they contact their lawyer to see what could be done.

Within a few weeks a surrogate female was found, and all the necessary contracts were drawn up and signed. Nine months later the couple become the proud parents of a bouncing baby boy.

As they gazed lovingly at their child through the nursery window, the two men noticed that while most of the other infants were occasionally crying and re-quiring a great deal of the nurse's attention, their son just lay in his crib smiling constantly. The gays become very distraught and signaled that they wanted to speak with the nurse. "Not to worry," she told them. "As soon as we remove the pacifier from your son's ass, he'll start acting just like the rest of them!"

18

One afternoon an attractive young girl got on a bus, spotted a good-looking guy sitting alone and sat down beside him. Just then the bus hit an enormous bump, and the seats bounced, causing her to release a loud fart. Out of embarrassment, she decided to start up a conversation with the fellow next to her. "Pardon me," she asked, "but do you have a newspaper I might borrow?"

"No, I don't," the young man replied. "But I'll tell you what. We'll be going through the park in a few minutes, and I'll grab you a handful of leaves."

19

A shipwrecked Polish sailor was marooned on a desert island with a female sheep and a male Doberman pinscher for companions. Before long the two animals grew quite attracted to each other. All went well until the man become unbearably horny and made a move for the ewe, which pissed off the dog. Baring its fangs, the Doberman place itself between the sheep and the ornery sailor.

Days later, spotting a raft on the horizon, the sailor swam out and found a beautiful girl onboard. He took her ashore and for the next few weeks fed and comforted her. "You've been so good to me," the grateful castaway said one morning. "I'd do absolutely *anything* to show my gratitude."

"Would you?" the sailor asked with a broad grin on his face. He excitedly unfastened the length of rope that held up his ragged pants and handed it to the girl.

"Here," the Polack muttered. "Use this as a leash and take that damn dog for a long walk!"

20

Q: What does an elephant use for a vibrator?
A: An epileptic.

21

There was this pro-football player named Sammy who always warmed the bench. Every game he'd put on his gear, smear his cheeks with charcoal, don his helmet and rush onto the field with his teammates. But play after play, game after game, year after year, he never saw any action.

One Sunday morning near the end of another idle season, Sammy was feeling pretty lousy. "Cathy," he asked his girlfriend, "do me a favor. Dress up in my uniform, smear your face, put on my helmet and sit on the bench for me. Nobody'll ever know."

Cathy agreed, and sure enough no one knew Sammy wasn't there. The first three quarters of the game were uneventful, but in the fourth quarter Sammy's team suffered a rash of serious injuries. With no one left on the bench, the coach yelled, "Sammy, get in there!"

Trembling, Cathy ran onto the field, crouched down

at the line of scrimmage and was knocked cold just after the ball was snapped. When she came to, the coach was vigorously massaging her pussy.

"Don't worry, Sammy," he said nervously. "Once we get your balls back in place, your cock'll pop right up!"

22

Q: If you're rating women, what's a Jewish 10?
A: A 3 with $7 million.

23

Q: What's a Mexican 10?
A: A 4 with a six-pack.

24

The HUSTLER Dictionary defines *pimp* as: a hooker booker.

25

An old man turned 115 and was being interviewed by a reporter for the local paper. During the interview the reporter noticed that the yard was full of children of all ages playing together. A very pretty girl of about

15 served the old man and the reporter, keeping them in fresh tea and running errands for them.

"Are these your grandkids?" the reporter asked.

"Naw, sir, they all be my younguns," the old man replied with a sly grin.

"Your kids?" said the reporter. "What about this beautiful young lady who keeps bringing us tea? Is she one of your children too?"

"Naw, sir," said the old man, "she be my wife."

"Your wife?" said the surprised reporter. "But she can't be more than 15 years old!"

"Thass right," said the old man with pride.

"Well surely you can't have a sex life, what with you being 115 and her only 15," the reporter remarked.

"Naw, sir," said the old man. "We have sex every night. Every night two of my boys helps me on it, and every morning six of my boys helps me off."

"Wait just one minute," said the newspaperman. "Why does it only take two of your boys to put you on, but it takes *six* of them to get you off?"

"Cause," the spry old man said with a balled fist, "I fights 'em!"

26

Q: What do you call a homosexual in jail?
A: Canned fruit.

27

One morning a milkman called on one of his regular customers and was surprised to see a white bedsheet with a hole in the middle hanging up in her living room. The housewife explained that she'd had a party the night before. They had played a game called "Who's Who," in which each of the men had put their equipment through the hole, and the women tried to guess their identity.

"Gee, that sounds like fun," said the milkman. "Sure wish I'd been there."

"You should have been," said the housewife. "Your name came up three times."

28

A man was speeding down the road with his deaf wife when he was stopped by a policeman. The cop walked up and asked to see the man's driver's license.

"What'd he say?" the woman yelled to her husband.

"He wants to see my driver's license," the guy shouted back at his spouse.

"Did you know you were going 100 mph?" the cop then asked the man.

"What'd he say?" shouted the lady.

"He said I was speeding," screamed the man.

The cop looked at the license, noted where the driver

was from and said, "Orlando, Florida, huh? I had the worst piece of ass I ever had in Orlando."

"What's he say?" shouted the lady.

"He thinks he knows you," her husband replied.

29

Q: Do you know how to starve a Puerto Rican to death?
A: Hide his food stamps under his work boots.

30

Jerome walked into a doctor's office and plopped his huge penis on the desk.

"What's the matter with that?" asked the MD.

"I don't know. Have a look at it."

The doctor got out his pencil, tried to pick up the penis, and the pencil broke. The physician finally lifted it with steel tongs, took a quick look and announced, "Ahh, you have VD!"

"That's impossible, doctor," said Jerome. "I can't have no VD. I use precautions."

"Look," said the doctor, "I'm damn fed up with you black folks coming in here and telling me you can't have VD. That is VD. Now what precautions have you been taking?"

"I been giving her a false name and address!"

31

The HUSTLER Dictionary defines *obscenity* as: anything a 70-year-old Republican can't do anymore.

32

A little white boy and a little black boy played jacks on the curb each morning in front of the Catholic Church. Every morning the priest would come out and say, "Good morning, boys."

"Good morning, Father," they'd say.

One morning, though, the priest came outside and found the little black boy all by himself.

"Good morning, son," the priest said.

"Good morning, Father," the youngster answered.

"By the way, my son," the priest remarked, "are you Catholic?"

"Hell, no," replied the little black boy, "it's tough enough being a nigger."

33

A wealthy older couple were dining in a posh restaurant when an attractive young woman approached the table, leaned over and kissed the older man passionately. The bimbo uttered, "Oh, Frank, thank you for that new mink. It's a beautiful stole." The sexy young thing then strutted away seductively. The old man's wife was stunned. Her mouth was hanging open, and a look of pure shock was evident on her face.

"Just who in hell was that, Frank?"

"That was my mistress, Helen," the old man replied coolly.

"Your mistress! Well then, I want a divorce," the old woman announced.

"All right, if that's what you wish, dearest, but think of the jewelry, the unlimited expense account, the trips around the world and all the other extravagant perks you'd be giving up if you divorce me."

His wife settled down, then she noticed an older couple that they knew dining at another table across the way. "Isn't that Victor and his wife over there? And who is that young hussy bending over Victor and kissing him?" the rich old man's wife asked.

"That's Victor's mistress," Frank replied.

"Oh," the old woman responded. "Our mistress is much better-looking."

34

Two Polacks entered an opium den, and as soon as they were in the door, they started picking up used hypodermic needles, so that they could shoot heroin. One junkie noticed what they were doing and said, "Hey, you're going to get AIDS doing that."

The Polacks answered, "Not a chance. We're wearing condoms."

35

Two guys were in a restaurant. One guy said to the other, "Hey, Jerry, isn't that your ex-wife, Donna, at the table over in the corner?"

"The bitch. Can you see who she's with?"

"The potted palm's blocking him."

"I don't care who she's with."

"Still smitten, eh?"

"Smitten, shitten, she's a bitch. I hope she's with Jack the Ripper—only he hasn't got a prayer."

"I admire your control. I'd be curious as hell. Oh he just leaned out. Looks like Henry."

"Henry?"

"Hey, Jerry, where you going?"

Jerry weaved his way through the tables to the other side of the restaurant, his stomach churning acid, and said, "Hello, Henry. Hello, Donna. How's that old, tired pussy of yours?"

Smiling, she gave him her best smirk and said, "Oh, just fine—once you get past the tiny bit that's been used!"

36

A man with a poodle went into a bar. After ordering a drink, he asked to buy some cigarettes, but was told that unfortunately, they had run out. So the man said, "That's all right, I'll just send my dog across the street to get some."

He searched through his pockets for the money and discovered that the smallest bill he had was a $20. He put it in the dog's mouth and told the dog, "Boy, run across the street and get me some cigarettes, and don't forget to bring back the change." Immediately the poodle ran out the front door.

A man sitting at the bar said to the dog's owner, "Say, that dog is really something! Is he really going to bring cigarettes back to you?"

"Sure," said the man. "He can do all sorts of stuff. He's an amazing dog."

Just then they heard tires screeching. The man looked up with fear in his eyes and said, "Oh, no!" He ran out to the street and saw a car stopped in front of the bar. Running around to the front of the car, he saw that it did not hit his dog after all but managed to stop just in time. The reason, however, for the sudden stop was to avoid hitting his dog, who was humping another poodle right in the middle of the road. "Hey," said the man to his dog, "what's going on? You never did anything like this before!"

The dog looked up. "I never had $20 before."

37

Two leprechauns knocked on the door of a convent. A nun answered and said, "How can I help you, little fellows?"

"Have you got any midget nuns?" asked one of the leprechauns.

"Midget nuns?" she said. "No, we don't."

The leprechaun said, "Oh, come on, you've got to have at least *one* midget nun."

"I'm sorry, little man," she told him, "but I'm afraid we don't."

The leprechaun started to get worked up and begged her. "Please," he said, "you've got to tell me that you have at least one midget nun!"

Finally his friend, the other leprechaun, elbowed him in the ribs and said, "You see, Jamie, I *told* you it was a penguin you screwed."

38

Two golfers were teeing off on the eighth hole when a funeral procession slowly went by the golf course. One golfer took off his hat and lowered his head. His partner asked, "Did you know the deceased?"

The other man replied, "Know her! I was married to her for twenty-five years."

39

A woman told her husband that he should experiment with eating her pussy because she'd heard it was a thrilling experience. The husband, who'd never done such a thing, went manfully to the task. The taste wasn't bad, but he found the smell overpowering. Suddenly the wife orgasmed and simultaneously emitted a tremendous fart. "Thank God," sighed the husband, "fresh air!"

40

A young priest happened to get a seat next to an old rabbi on a plane flying across the country. While waiting on the runway, the priest began talking to the rabbi. "You know," he said, "you really should think about becoming a Roman Catholic. It is the best religion of all." As the plane took off, the eager young priest continued, trying to talk the old rabbi into joining the Roman Catholic faith. Suddenly, the plane went into a tailspin and crashed. The priest was miraculously thrown from the plane. As he looked back at the wreckage, he saw the old rabbi pick himself up and make the sign of the cross. The priest ran up to him, saying, "Oh, thank heavens I got to talk to you in time. As we were going down, you saw that what I was saying was right, and you decided to convert!"

"Vat are you talking about?" asked the old rabbi.

"As you stepped from the wreckage," said the priest, "I saw you make the sign of the cross!"

"Vat cross?" said the rabbi. "I vas checking my spectacles, testicles, vallet and vatch."

41

A flea was on the beach in Florida. He set up his little beach chair and was sunbathing with his little reflector when a friend of his happened to walk by. The other flea looked really beat up. The flea sunbathing looked up and said, "Hey, what happened to you? You look terrible."

"Oh," said the other flea, "I had an awful trip down here. I hitched a ride in a guy's mustache, who happened to be driving a motorcycle. It was just terrible! The wind was blowing me all over the place!"

"Well," said the flea sitting in the sun, "you did it the wrong way. Next time go to the stewardesses' lounge at the airport, hop up on the toilet seat, and when one of the stewardesses sits down, jump up into her pubic hair. It's warm, it smells good and you ride in style!"

So the next year the same flea was on the beach with his little reflector, sunbathing, when he looked up and saw his friend. The other flea was again all mangled and beaten up. "Hey," he said, "what happened to you? Last year I thought I told you how to make this trip the right way."

"Yeah, well," said his friend, "I went to the airport, like you said. I went to the stewardesses' lounge. I hopped up on the toilet seat. A stewardess sat down. I jumped up in her pubic hair. The next thing I knew, I was in this guy's mustache on a motorcycle."

42

A man and a woman were stranded on a life raft after their boat sunk. One morning the woman awoke to find the man holding a knife under his limp prick. "What are you doing?" she gasped.

"I can't help it," the man said, "I've just got to have something to eat!"

"Wait," the woman pleaded. "Let me play with it for a while, then there will be enough for both of us!"

43

After five years in prison, an ex-con was released. He called his wife and told her to get ready to make mad, passionate love because he was on his way home. A short time later, the eager wife, clad only in a sheer black negligee, opened the front door to see her husband standing there on the porch, holding a bottle of whiskey in each hand. "Honey, are you ready?" she asked.

"Am I ready? What the hell do you think I rang the doorbell with?"

44

Q: How do yuppies wean their children?
A: They fire the maid.

45

Jesus and St. Peter were standing at the Pearly Gates when someone arrived fresh from Earth. "What's your name?" Jesus asked.

"Joseph," said the man.

"What was your trade?" asked Jesus.

"Carpenter," replied the man.

Jesus paused for a moment. "Did you have a son?"

"Yes."

"Did he disappear?" asked Jesus.

"Yes."

"Did he have holes in his feet and hands?"

"Yes, he did."

"Father!" shouted Jesus.

"Pinnochio!" shouted the carpenter.

46

Two little, old black ladies were rocking back and forth in their chairs on the front porch of the rest home. Ethel said to Mabel, "Do you 'member all of them dances we used to do?"

"Yep."

"The waltz?"

"Yep."

"The minuet?" Ethel asked.

"Hell," Mabel replied, "I can't 'member the men I *fucked*, let alone the men I *et*!"

47

The HUSTLER Dictionary defines *AIDS* as: the fucking you get from the fucking you got.

48

A guy walked into a bar carrying an octopus, sat down and ordered a beer. The bartender came over, set it down and said, "What's with your octopus?"

The guy said, "This is my famous octopus; he can play any musical instrument ever made."

"Oh, yeah," said the bartender, "a beer says he can't play that piano!"

The octopus jumped on the piano seat and rattled off

some ragtime. "Pretty good," said the bartender. "How about this trumpet?"

"Okay," the guy said. The octopus blew some Herb Alpert.

"Wow," said the bartender, "but how about these bagpipes?" The octopus jumped on the bagpipes, rolled down to the end of the bar, stopped and rolled back to the other end, but no music was heard.

The bartender said, "I got you on this one."

"Not yet," the guy said. "When he figures out he can't fuck it, he'll play it."

49

Q: How can you tell when you are getting old?

A: When you have dry dreams and wet farts.

50

A widow and a widower went to the same park near their retirement center each day for two years. They had noticed each other, but had never spoken. Finally, the widower decided he'd make the first move and said hello to her. For several weeks they met at the park, and their conversations went well; so the widower asked the widow to have dinner with him. She readily accepted his invitation. The relationship progressed, and the widower asked the widow to move in with him. The widow hesitated for a moment, then asked, "What will we do about the rent?"

"Oh, we'll share it," he replied.

"What about the food and utilities?" she asked.

The widower replied, "We can share those too."

Still concerned by the arrangement, the widow asked, "What about sex?"

"Oh, infrequently," he responded quickly.

The widow then asked, "Is that one word or two?"

51

After driving his car into a utility pole at the corner of Constitution and Independence Streets, Leroy ran to a nearby phone to call for help. "You gotta hurry," he told the ambulance dispatcher. "My brother is knocked out and bleeding to death."

"Where are you?" asked the dispatcher.

"Corner of Independence and Constitution," said Leroy.

"Can you spell that please?" asked the dispatcher.

"Lessee . . . I-n-d-p— No. C-o-n-t—hey, just a minute," said Leroy, running to the corner. After staring at the sign for a while, he ran back to the phone. "Hello, this is Leroy again. Look, I'm fixin' to drag this motherfucker to First and Main."

52

After working and drinking beer all day on the construction site, Bill really had to take a piss. Being a little light-headed, he wandered by accident into the explosives-storage room. Not finding a light, Bill lit a match, and blew the place sky-high. Bill's boss came running over and heard Bill mutter, "My God, where's my hand?"

"Forget your damn hand, man! We have to get you to a hospital; your legs are missing," said the panic-stricken boss.

At the hospital, Bill kept screaming, "My hand . . . my hand . . . get me my hand!"

The doctor told him, "Listen, man, your legs are gone, and you're bleeding uncontrollably. What's so important about your goddamn hand?"

Bill looked at the doctor and screamed, "My dick is still in it!"

53

Q: What do you call an anorexic with a yeast infection?
A: A quarter-pounder with cheese.

54

The Pope and the archbishop were talking, and the archbishop happened to mention that he had heard a good joke the day before. The Pope said, "Oh, I like jokes—let me hear it."

The archbishop said, "Okay, this is a good one! There were two Polacks walking down the street, and—"

Immediately the Pope interrupted him. "Excuse me, but are you aware of the fact that I happen to be Polish?" he asked.

The archbishop was shocked. "Oh, my gosh," he said, "that's right! I'm really sorry." The archbishop then said very slowly, "There . . . were . . . two . . . Polacks . . . walking . . . down . . . the . . . street . . ."

55

The HUSTLER Dictionary defines *eternity* as: the length of time between when you come and when she leaves.

56

A cab driver saw a woman hailing him at 39th Street and 11th Avenue. He pulled over and was surprised when she got in and sat down beside him on the front seat. She told him her address, and they drove off. When they arrived at her destination, the cab driver pulled over and shut off the meter. "Okay," he said, "that will be $4.60, please."

The woman looked over and said to him, "I don't have any money," pulling her skirt up to her waist, "but maybe this will take care of it."

The cabby looked down and said, "Gee, lady, don't you have anything smaller?"

57

One day a kindergarten teacher decided to test her students on animal sounds. Calling on little Mary, she asked, "Mary, what does the cow say?"

"Mooo," answered Mary.

"Very good," said the teacher. "Now, Johnny, what does the sheep say?"

"Baaa," replied Johnny.

Then the teacher asked little Leroy, "What does the pig say, Leroy?"

Leroy thought, then said, "Freeze, nigger!"

58

An American, a German and a Russian were talking about their traveling habits. The American said, "Well, when I'm at home, I'm satisfied with my Chevy. But when I travel abroad, I must show off in a Cadillac."

The German said, "Being at home, my Volkswagen is good enough for me. But if I take a trip, it must be in the Mercedes."

Then the Russian added dryly, "As for my nation, in our homeland we are pretty satisfied with our Volgas. And as for the trips to foreign countries, we usually travel in tanks."

59

Q: Why do bikers always name their dicks?

A: Because they don't want a stranger making 95 percent of their decisions.

60

A truck driver picked up one of those long-haired androgynous types that are so in vogue these days. After about an hour of silence, the hitchhiker said, "Well, aren't you going to ask me?"

"Ask you what?" the truck driver replied.

"Whether I'm a boy or a girl?"

"It don't make any difference," answered the trucker. "I'm fucking you anyway."

61

A visitor found himself at the entrance of a South Central Los Angeles bar. He asked the doorman, "Is there any cover?"

"No," the doorman replied, "we just duck behind the bar."

62

During an exclusive interview with a reporter for a national news magazine, Richard Nixon readily offered his charitable, enlightened views on domestic policy and foreign relations. Finally, the discussion turned to his own political career, and the ex-president revealed that he was considering running for the nation's highest office again.

"Honestly?" the stunned reporter asked.

"Hell, no," Nixon replied. "The same as last time."

63

Two men in Ireland were digging a ditch, which happened to be directly across from a brothel. Suddenly, they saw a Protestant minister walk up to the front door of the bordello, look around, and then go inside.

"Ah, will you look at that?" said one ditchdigger to the other. "Begorra, what is our world coming to when the men of the cloth are visiting such places?"

A few minutes later, a rabbi walked up to the door and quietly slipped inside. "Do you believe that? Why, it's no wonder the young people of today are so confused, with the example the clergymen set for them."

Next, a Catholic priest quickly entered the whorehouse. "Ah, what a pity," said the ditchdigger to his buddy. "One of the poor girls must be dying."

64

A man went to see his doctor because he was having sexual problems with the missus. After listening to his lament, the physician said, "It sounds like a case of simple bedroom boredom. Let me tell you about a little game my wife and I used to play to spice up our sex life. She would sit at one end of the bed with her legs spread, and I'd sit at the other," the doctor continued. "I'd throw grapes at her pussy, and all the ones she caught I'd eat right out of her box. Then she'd throw doughnuts at me and munch every one of 'em that got caught on my dick."

The man got terribly excited and rushed to the phone to call his wife. "Honey," he said, "our problems are solved. I'm on my way home now. Before I get there, though, I want you to go out and buy a box of Cheerios and a dozen cantaloupes."

65

Q: What's the difference between a woman and a toilet?

A: A toilet doesn't follow you around after you use it.

66

A well-stacked redhead stormed into police headquarters and shouted to the desk sergeant that a man had grabbed and raped her while she was walking through the park.

"What did he look like?" the desk sergeant asked.

"I don't really know," the girl replied.

"Lady, it's in the middle of the afternoon on a clear, sunny day," the sergeant said in an exasperated voice. "How could a man grab and rape you without you see what he looked like?"

"Well, for one thing," the redhead answered, "I always close my eyes when I'm being screwed."

67

In an effort to get rid of hookers the police clamped down and arrested any woman seen working the streets that night. The line to the jail was so long, it went around the block. An old lady passing by spotted her granddaughter and asked what the line was for. The girl, not wanting her granny to know about her work, said free oranges were being handed out.

"Oh, good," said the old lady, who immediately went to the back of the line. After a while she reached the front and was amazed to find herself in the police department. Equally amazed was the desk sergeant, who blew his cool when he saw the old lady.

"Tell me, madam," he said with an air of surprise, "aren't you a little old for this?"

"Don't you believe it," said the old lady. "I take my teeth out and suck 'em dry."

68

Two hunters were forced by a storm to seek shelter in a house occupied by a farmer's widow. When the hunters met again the following season, one asked, "Did you screw that old bag we stayed with last year?"

"Sure did," admitted the other.

"And you used my name and told her you were me?"

"Yeah, I did that too," laughed his hunting pal. "Didn't knock her up, did I?"

"No, no," smiled his friend. "It's just that she died yesterday and left me her house and $100,000!"

69

Q: What's the difference between a circumcision and a crucifixion?

A: In a circumcision they don't throw the whole Jew away.

70

A couple appeared before the judge in a divorce proceeding. "What are your grounds?" he asked.

"Cruel and inhuman punishment," the woman said. "He tied me to the bed, then forced me to sing the national anthem while he peed on me."

"That's horrible," the magistrate muttered.

"Yeah," the woman said. "He knows how much I hate to sing!"

71

The circus was coming to town, and all four elephants were walking in traditional fashion, each one grasping with his trunk the tail of the elephant in front. They reached some railroad tracks and almost crossed them safely when a train hit the last one.

A few months later the railroad company received a bill for the loss of four pachyderms. "But we killed only one," said the spokesman.

"Yes," said the circus owner, "but you tore the asses out of the other three."

72

Lisa and Jeff were celebrating their tenth wedding anniversary. "You can have anything you want for a present," announced Lisa.

"How about a blowjob?" Jeff asked.

That night in bed Lisa, doing it for the first time, made a great effort to please her mate. When she sensed he was getting close to a climax, she asked, "Honey, what do I do when you come?"

"How do I know?! I'm not a cocksucker!"

73

After experiencing severe menstrual pain for several months, a black woman decided to see her gynecologist. "What seems to be the problem?" he asked.

"It's mah period, Doc. It's been causin' me pain."

"And how long have you been having this problem?" he inquired.

"Oh, 'bout three or four months," the woman replied.

The MD shook his head, thought for a minute and then asked, "Well, tell me about the flow. Is there anything unusual about it?"

The woman looked puzzled and stared at the doctor for a long time. Finally, being totally perplexed, she said, "I don't know what that has to do with any of this, but mah flo' is linoleum."

74

An American wrestler was listening to his manager's advice about his next match. "The guy's an Australian who has this lock-hold that he calls a 'Kangaroo Hold.' If he gets you in this hold, you're fucked. It can't be broken." The manager demonstrated the hold and the ways to block it.

The match started, and immediately the American boy got locked into the dreaded Kangaroo Hold. The manager threw his hands over his eyes in utter despair. Suddenly, the crowd went wild. The manager looked up and saw the referee holding up the American's hand in victory. Back in the dressing room the manager said, "I didn't see what happened. How in the hell did you break that fuckin' hold?"

"Well," the wrestler said, "he had me all twisted up, and I looked up and saw this pair of balls hanging in front of my face; so I bit 'em. You'd be surprised how strong you can get when you bite your own nuts!"

75

One night in bed a man told his wife that he didn't want to make love to her anymore because her cunt was too big.

"Not anymore," his wife said proudly. "I've been doing exercises to slim up my pussy. Here," she added, grabbing both of her husband's hands and shoving them up her twat.

"Now what?" he asked.

"Try to clap your hands," the wife said.

"I can't."

"See?"

76

Q: What does it say on a black epileptic's medical ID bracelet?

A: I'm not break-dancing!

77

A guy wearing a ski mask ran into an empty bar, pulled out a gun and told the bartender, "Put your hands up!"

"Don't shoot," the man pleaded. "I've got a wife and kids."

"Shut up," the crook muttered. "Just empty the cash register."

"All right," begged the barkeep. "Just don't shoot."

The robber took the money, pointed the gun at the bartender's head and said, "Get down on your knees, cocksucker, and blow me."

"Anything," cried the bartender. "Just don't shoot me." He started blowing the intruder, but soon the excited bandit dropped his gun. The bartender picked it up and handed it back to the crook. "Hold the gun!" he snapped. "One of my friends might walk in!"

78

Q: What do you get when you cross a black with a Jew?

A: A janitor at a law firm.

79

The HUSTLER Dictionary defines *chamber of commerce* as: a whore's pussy.

80

The HUSTLER Dictionary defines *vagina* as: a box a penis comes in.

81

The HUSTLER Dictionary defines *Polish Jacuzzi* as: a 55-gallon water drum with an eggbeater.

82

Two braggarts sat in a bar engaging in lively conversation. "When I was hunting for grizzly bear last year, I had a very close encounter," one boasted. "As I came across a hill, I saw the bear of my dreams. It stood a solid twelve feet high. In my excitement I took aim and fired, but I only grazed the monstrous creature! Scared to death about what it might do to me, I ran like hell. And do you know that I'd outrun the bear by a distance of two miles by the time I reached my cabin?"

The second braggart looked suspiciously at the first. "I find that impossible to believe," he said. "A wounded bear can run as fast as a race horse."

"Yeah, but I had an advantage," the first fellow answered. "I was running on flat ground, and the bear was running through three inches of shit!"

83

A furious pounding in a hotel room late at night awakened a number of guests. The hotel detective was called, and he let himself into the room. Inside, he found an elderly man banging away on the bathroom door with both fists as he cursed.

"Stop that," the detective said. "You're disturbing the whole hotel."

"Damn the hotel," the elderly man spat. "It's the first erection I've had in years, and my wife fell asleep in the bathtub!"

84

On the night of her honeymoon a bride slipped into a flimsy bit of satin and crawled into bed, only to find that her husband had settled down on the couch. When she asked why he was apparently not going to make love to her, he replied, "Because it's Lent."

"Why, that's the most ridiculous thing I've ever heard," she cried, almost in tears. "Lent to whom and for how long?"

85

A young businessman appeared at a bus stop, where he met an older man and a rather large bulldog. "Does your dog bite?" he asked the older gentleman.

"No, my dog is real friendly," came the reply.

On hearing this, the young man started to pet the animal. To his shock and horror, the dog bit him several times and tore the sleeve of his suit to shreds. "I thought you said your dog was friendly!" the businessman exclaimed.

"He is," the old man replied, "but that ain't my dog!"

86

"What's the trouble, mac?" the sympathetic bartender questioned the morose drinker. "Why don't you tell me about it?"

"I got caught today screwing my next-door neighbor," groaned the fellow.

"Hey, that's heavy! Who caught you," pursued the bartender, "her husband?"

"No," moaned the drinker, "the guy's wife."

87

Two Polish carpenters were framing a new house when the older one spotted the younger one throwing nails away. He'd hammer one into the lumber, then toss the next nail down. Soon there were nails all over the ground.

"Are you crazy?" asked the older Pole as he climbed down from his ladder. "Why are you throwing those good nails away?"

"I can't hit them with the hammer is why," said the younger one. "The head is on the wrong end of the nail."

"There's nothing wrong with these nails, you idiot," said the older carpenter as he began to pick them up. "They go on the other side of the house!"

88

Two drunks staggered out of a bar and inadvertently began walking down a railroad track. About an hour later one said to the other, "This is the longest stairway I've ever been on."

"It's not the distance that bothers me," the other drunk replied. "These low handrails are killing me!"

89

When a persistent pain in his rectum didn't ease after several days, a gay lumberjack made an appointment to see his proctologist. During the examination the physician was shocked to find a bouquet lodged up the man's ass.

"Where in the hell did these come from?" the astonished doctor asked as he removed the flowers.

"I'm not sure," said the lumberjack, smiling. "Why don't you read the card?"

90

A sweet young thing was taken to a fancy restaurant by her elderly employer. After a few cocktails, the young lady ordered a pâté de foie gras, an endive salad, chateaubriand, dessert and coffee, along with the most expensive bottle of French champagne the establishment served.

The old gentleman stared quizzically at her. "Your mother feeds you this way?" he asked.

"No," replied the young lady, "but my mother doesn't want to fuck me either."

91

Johnny came running home from school and cried, "Dad, I don't understand all of the words the big kids use."

"Well, sit down then, son, and I'll explain them to you," his father said.

"Okay, Dad, what's a pussy?"

"You've seen your mother naked?" the father replied. "A pussy is the clump of hair between her legs."

"Well, then," continued Johnny, "what's a bitch?"

"That, my son," answered his father, "would be the rest of her."

92

The HUSTLER Dictionary defines *German tampon* as: a twatstika.

93

Q: What new use have West Virginia boys found for sheep?

A: They get wool from them.

94

It had taken a while for the man to persuade his wife to let him make love to her. She hadn't been very cooperative during the act and, now that it was over, she snapped, "You're lucky, Ralph, that I don't make you pay me what I'm worth for submitting to this!"

"I sure am, Blanche," sighed the husband, "because if I did that, I'd probably be arrested for violating the minimum-wage law."

95

A young rape victim was telling the cops her story. The detective asked her what the rapist looked like. "I don't know," she replied, "but he was from Texas."

"Was he tall, short, black, white, Mexican—what?"

"I don't know," the woman replied, "but he was from Texas."

"Did you see him at all?" the flustered cop inquired.

"No, but he was from Texas!" the woman insisted.

"If you didn't see him at all, how'd you know he was from Texas?" the detective prodded.

"Because the guy had an 8-inch belt buckle and a 4-inch prick!"

96

One afternoon a little farm girl answered the door. The caller, a rather troubled-looking, middle-aged man, asked to see her father.

"If you've come about the bull," she said, "he's $50. We have the papers, and he's guaranteed."

"Young lady," the man said, "I want to see your father."

"If that's too much for you, mister," the little girl added, "we've got us another bull that goes for $25, and he's guaranteed too, but he doesn't have any papers."

"I'm not here for a bull," said the man angrily. "I want to talk to your father about Elmer. Your brother's gotten my daughter in trouble."

"Oh, I'm sorry," said the little girl, "but you'll have to see Pa about that too. I don't know what he charges for Elmer."

97

It was six o'clock in the morning at Marine boot camp in mid-February. The temperature was about ten degrees below zero.

The sergeant said, "All right, scumbags, fall in outside, stark naked! And stand close enough to make the guy in front of you smile!" Despite the freezing weather, the Marines did as commanded.

Now the sergeant said, "Okay, loosen ranks." Everyone stepped back a bit, and the sergeant started walking among the men. He was carrying a riding crop in his hand. Suddenly, he smacked one of the men across the chest. "Did that hurt, soldier?"

The soldier answered, "No, sir!"

The sergeant then asked, "Why not?"

"Because I'm a U.S. Marine, sir!" came the answer.

The sergeant nodded and walked around to the next row. Presently, he smacked another soldier across the ass. "Did that hurt, soldier?"

The soldier answered, "No, sir!"

The sergeant asked, "Why not?"

"Because I'm a U.S. Marine, sir!" came the expected response.

The sergeant nodded again and mumbled, "Good platoon." He started down the next row and found one of the soldiers had a huge erection. He walked around it, stared at it, then turned and *whack!* hit it with the riding crop. He bellowed, "Did that hurt, soldier?"

The soldier answered, "No, sir!"

The sergeant asked, "Why not?"

"Because it belongs to the guy in back of me, sir!"

98

Q: Did you hear about the Puerto Rican who refused to smoke crack?

A: He was into classic coke.

99

A carpet layer was installing new wall-to-wall carpeting in the family room of a home. He'd had a little too much to drink the night before; so he was a bit disoriented as he worked. Finally, he finished and stepped back to inspect the job. To his dismay, he noticed a lump right in the middle of the floor.

The thought of tearing up all the carpet turned his stomach. He searched his pockets for a brief time, looking for a smoke. Then he realized his pack of cigarettes was missing. He checked his toolbox and jacket, but the cigarettes were not to be found.

Then he had an idea. He got out a hammer and began smashing the lump. It took quite a while, but finally the lump was so flattened that it was barely noticeable. Satisfied, he carried his gear back out to the truck.

His pack of cigarettes was on the front seat. Undaunted, he headed back toward the house. As he walked in the front door, he heard a little boy say, "Mommy, have you seen my kitten?"

100

Roy and his buddy, Donny, were duck hunting. Roy pointed off to the left and snapped his fingers, and his dog, Warren, ran off into the marsh. Momentarily, Warren returned. He had a twig in his mouth, and he started shaking his head and humping wildly on Donny's leg.

Donny screamed, "Roy, call your dog off! This old hound of yours has finally lost his mind!"

Roy answered, "Like hell he has! Can't you see he's trying to tell you that over to the left there are more fucking ducks than you can shake a stick at?"

101

A hit-and-run victim slowly got to his feet. "My mother-in-law just tried to run me over," he explained to the policeman.

"But how do you know that it was your mother-in-law?" asked the officer.

The man answered: "I'd recognize that laugh anywhere!"

102

Two men and a woman were stranded on an island. After two weeks, the woman was so ashamed of what she was doing, she killed herself.

After two more weeks, the men were so ashamed, they finally buried her.

After two more weeks, the men were so ashamed of what they were doing, they dug her back up.

103

A man and a woman were sitting in a bar. The man was depressed because his wife had just divorced him. Likewise, the woman's husband had just divorced her, and she was very depressed.

The man noticed the woman and started talking to her. After a few drinks she admitted to the man that she was sad because her divorce was just finalized and that her husband had dumped her because she was too kinky for him.

"Really," he answered, "that's the same reason my wife just divorced me."

Since they seemed to have so much in common, they decided to go back to her place and fuck with unbridled abandon. After about fifteen minutes the woman emerged from the bathroom decked out in full leather, whip in one hand, chains in the other. She found the man stretched out naked on her couch, smoking a cigarette.

"What's so kinky about that?" she snarled.

"Well, I don't know what you consider to be kinky," he answered, "but I just fucked your cat and shit in your purse."

104

The HUSTLER Dictionary defines *G-string* as: anal floss.

105

A high-school student working part-time in a rural pharmacy was left temporarily in charge while the pharmacist ran an errand. Upon the pharmacist's return, he asked the young man if there had been any customers.

"One," the young man replied. "A man wanted something for a cough."

"And what did you recommend?" the pharmacist asked.

"Castor oil," the young man answered.

"Castor oil! Castor oil isn't any good for a cough!"

"You want to bet?" he replied. "That man is standing out there on the corner, and he's too scared to cough!"

106

Q: What's the difference between lawyers and vultures?
A: Lawyers accumulate frequent-flyer miles.

107

The biker was testifying in court on behalf of a friend, and suddenly the prosecuting attorney jumped up and demanded, "Isn't it true that you were paid $5,000 to throw this case?"

The biker just stared out the courtroom windows and said nothing. The prosecuting attorney repeated the question and was again ignored. Finally the judge leaned over and admonished the biker, "You will answer the question, young man."

"Aw, shit, Judge, I'm sorry," replied the biker. "I thought he was talking to you."

108

A salesman pulled off the highway and stopped at a restaurant for a quick bite. Before leaving, he visited the restroom and noticed a box attached to the wall with a hole in it and a sign reading, "Let me be your wife— 25 cents." Intrigued, the fellow inserted a quarter and slipped his dick into the hole.

A few minutes later, he came crashing through the restroom door, screaming in pain. The alarmed restaurant manager rushed over and asked him, "Sir, what's the matter?"

The salesman cried, "I tried your 'Let me be your wife' machine, and I'm suing you."

"Didn't it work?"

"Oh, it worked all right," he groaned. "I just didn't know it was going to sew a damn button on my dick."

109

The HUSTLER Dictionary defines *hair lip* as: someone
who doesn't wipe his mouth after eating pussy.

110

On the night of their wedding anniversary, Mike's wife
was awakened by Mike's sudden crying fit. "What's
the matter, darling?" she asked.

Pulling himself together, Mike said, "Do you remember the night your father caught us screwing in
your backyard?"

"Yes," she replied, "of course, I remember."

"Do you also remember how he forced us to get married, threatening to have me arrested and sent to prison
for twenty-five years?"

"Yes, I remember, honey, but why are you crying
about this now?"

"I just realized I'd be getting out tomorrow!" Mike
wailed.

111

Sunday was to be the day of Phil's wedding, and he and
his father were enjoying a nightcap together. Lifting his
glass in a toast to his father, Phil asked, "Any advice
before I take the big step, Dad?"

"Yes," the father said. "Two things: First, insist on having one night out each week with the boys. Second, don't waste it on the boys."

112

A woman was lying in bed late one night, unable to sleep. Finally, she woke her husband up and said, "Murray, I've got to know. If I died, would you marry again?"

"I suppose so," he replied.

"Would you sleep with her in this bed?" the wife asked.

"It's the only bed in the house," the husband answered.

"Would you make love to her?"

"Honey," the husband replied, "of course—we'd be married. Now, go to sleep."

"One more question," she said. "Would you let her drive my car?"

"No," the husband answered. "She doesn't know how to drive a stick shift."

113

A drunk was walking down the street with one foot on the curb and one foot in the gutter. A cop stopped him and said, "I've got to take you in, sir. You're totally drunk."

The guy asked, "Officer, are you absolutely sure that I'm drunk?"

"Yes, I'm sure," answered the cop. "You're stoned drunk."

Relieved, the drunk answered, "Thank goodness! I thought I was a cripple!"

114

Two hookers were sitting in a bar discussing business one night. Said one, "God, business has been so slow for me lately. How about yours?"

"Not too good for me either, I'm afraid," the other one answered. "To make matters worse, a guy came in last night and asked me, 'How much?' I told him that for $100 he could fuck me all night. Then he told me that he only had $20. So I told him that all he would get was a handjob. He thought that was okay; so we went up to a room. Well, when he stripped down, I discovered that he had a 14-inch dick!"

"Cool," said the first hooker. "So what'd you do?"

She answered, "I lent him the 80 bucks!"

115

Q: What's the difference between a woman with PMS and a pit bull?

A: Jewelry.

116

Not realizing that the in-flight P.A. system was still on after takeoff, the pilot remarked to his copilot, "Man, all I need is to take a healthy shit and then get a blowjob from the stewardess, and I'll be set."

When the message was loudly broadcast over the speakers, the shocked stewardess hurried forward to warn the pilot.

As she rushed up the aisles, an old woman stopped her and whispered, "No need to rush, dearie. He said he was going to take a shit first."

117

The HUSTLER Dictionary defines *wake-up erection* as: morning thickness.

118

The HUSTLER Dictionary defines *nudist colony* as: a place where men and women air their differences.

119

When Randy came home at four in the morning, he found his wife in bed with another man. She screamed at her husband, "Just where have you been until four this morning?"

He shouted back, "Just who is that man?"

"Don't try to change the subject," she answered.

120

A man was recovering from a heart attack. His doctor told him, "No more drinking, smoking or carousing for you."

"How about sex?" asked the patient.

"Well, okay, I guess so. But only with your wife—I don't want you getting excited."

121

The HUSTLER Dictionary defines *foreplay* as: a premature ejaculator's nightmare.

122

A young farmer was having trouble with his wife. He went to see the family doctor, who told him, "You've got to be more loving and affectionate. When you feel romantic, go up and give her a big kiss."

"But, Doc, I can't. I'm out working in the fields from dawn to dark."

The doctor thought a moment, then said, "I've got it. Take your shotgun with you. Whenever you're in the mood for some loving, fire a blast into the air. When she hears it, she can come running."

The farmer agreed to follow the advice and didn't see the doctor for four moths. Then the farmer appeared at the office, depressed again.

"What's wrong?" the doctor asked. "Did you follow my advice?"

"Yes, indeed," the farmer said. "Worked great for a while. Then hunting season started a month ago, and I haven't seen her since!"

123

A man with leukemia insisted upon telling all his acquaintances that he had AIDS. Finally, a friend stopped him and said, "I know you've got leukemia, and that's plenty bad, but why are you telling everyone you've got AIDS?"

"Because when I die, I don't want anyone fucking my wife."

124

Q: What is the difference between a pussy and a cunt?
A: A pussy is soft, warm and inviting. A cunt is the woman who owns it.

125

The HUSTLER Dictionary defines *disgusting* as: anything that's too embarrassing to admit being turned-on by.

126

A woman with fourteen children, ages 1 through 14, decided to sue her husband for divorce on grounds of desertion.

"When did he desert you?" the judge asked.

"Thirteen years ago," she replied.

"If he left thirteen years ago, where did all the children come from?"

"Well," said the woman, "he kept coming back to say he was sorry."

127

A priest, a minister and a rabbi were all enjoying a beer together when a fly landed right in the priest's glass. The priest dipped his finger in the glass and pulled the fly out. He then shook the fly off of his finger, saying, "Be gone into the air, little creature of God."

A few minutes later, the fly returned, this time landing in the minister's glass. The minister did the same as the priest, saying to the fly, "Be free and go on your way, little bug."

The fly was mighty persistent, though, and soon he

was back at the table and nosediving into the rabbi's beer. The rabbi jerked the fly out of the glass and tossed it violently into the air, screaming, "Spit it out! Spit it out!"

128

Strolling down a residential street, a psychic casually mentioned to his buddy, "In the house over there lives a woman who's on the rag today."

"You can't possibly know that," the friend replied incredulously.

"Wanna bet? Just ring the door bell and ask. Hundred dollars to you if I'm wrong. Two hundred to me if I'm right," responded the psychic.

The doubting friend agreed and rang the bell. No response. He rang again—nothing. Only after several attempts was the door answered by a man dressed only in boxer shorts.

"Excuse me, sir," the friend politely inquired, "does your wife happen to have her period today?"

The man in the door was visibly embarrassed. He wiped his mouth and answered, "Well, yeah . . . does it show?"

129

A lawyer croaked and went to heaven. As he approached the Pearly Gates, he saw a band playing and thousands of angels cheering. Saint Peter himself rushed over to shake the shark's hand. "This is quite a reception," marveled the new arrival.

"You're special," explained Saint Peter. "We've never had anyone live to 135 before."

"But I'm only 85," said the lawyer.

Then Saint Peter thought for a moment. "Oh," he said. "We must have added up your billing hours."

130

A black man died and went up to heaven. As he tried to stroll through the Pearly Gates, he was stopped by Saint Peter. "Just a minute, mister. What did you do in your earthly life that was deserving of eternal life in heaven?"

"Why, Saint Peter," he said, "I'll have you know that I went up to the Imperial Wizard of the Ku Klux Klan, ripped off his hood and told him to his face he was a scum-sucking racist."

"And when did you do this?" snorted an unbelieving Saint Peter.

"Oh, about a minute ago," replied the black man.

131

Q: Why do Jewish men like to watch porn movies backward?

A: They like to see the part where the hooker gives the money back.

132

After meeting at a bar, the couple returned to the woman's apartment for a nightcap. Before long, things turned passionate, and the pair headed for the bedroom, clothes flying as they went.

Ten minutes later, the woman shot straight up in bed. "Oh, my God!" she cried. "My husband's coming!"

"Shit!" the fellow exclaimed, desperately trying to find his trousers. "Where's the back door?"

"There *is* no back door."

"Well," he said, "where would you like one?"

133

Q: How can you tell when Orientals have moved into the neighborhood?

A: The Mexicans get car insurance.

134

Two guys were sitting at a bar talking about their wives. "My old lady is so ugly," one said, "that the beauty parlor told her there was nothing more they could do."

"You think that's bad?" the other man asked. "I took my wife to a plastic surgeon and asked him what he could do to make my wife look better. The only thing he could think of was adding a tail."

135

Q: Why did the hillbilly walk his kid to elementary
   school every day?
A: They were in the same grade.

136

A flat-chested girl with limited funds went to a surgeon
to get her breasts enlarged. The surgeon performed the
cheapest procedure possible, which entailed the girl
flapping her arms up and down to enlarge her breasts.

Afterward, the girl went to the local bar to see what
kind of reaction her new tits would get. She decided to
flash them at a man who was standing alone in the corner. As she walked toward him, she pumped her tits as
big as they'd go. "Hi," she said coyly, "don't I know
you?"

"No," he answered, furiously pumping his legs together, "but I think we have the same doctor."

137

A Texas oil man was traveling across the desert in
Israel. Dying of thirst, he happened upon a small,
wooden shack, the only building he'd seen for a hundred miles. He aimed the Mercedes toward the driveway, got out, walked up to the door and knocked. A
little old Jewish man peeked out.

The Texan roared, "Can a cowboy get some water?"
"Sure. Vhy not?"

The little Jewish man walked the Texan around the back to the well and poured him some water from a bucket. As the Texan drank, he looked over the tiny property and remarked, "How big a spread you got here, son?"

The little Jewish man said, "Vell, mine property line goes from dat rock over dere to dat iron pipe, den it comes cross da front of mine house to dat date tree, unt den back to da chicken coop . . . unt finally, back to de rock."

Arrogantly, the Texan smiled and said, "Why, back in Texas, ma spread's so big, I climb into my car at daybreak and don't get out of my driveway until two o'clock."

The little Jewish man looked up at the Texan and said: "I know vhat you mean—I had a car like dat once too."

138

Q: What do you call two women in a freezer?
A: Cold cunts.

139

A man walked into his supervisor's office after being turned down for another raise and said, "You know, you don't ever have to worry about getting hemorrhoids."

"Why's that?" asked his boss.

"Because when God made you, he made the perfect asshole!"

140

The HUSTLER Dictionary defines *X-rated movie* as: boy-meats-girl story.

141

A suburban woman and three friends were playing bridge one evening. When the hostess's husband came into the room and announced that he was going to bed, she unzipped his fly, took out his penis, kissed it and said good night.

The other three women were dumbstruck. "Helen, that's the most disgusting thing I've ever seen!" one exclaimed.

"You wouldn't think it was so disgusting," she replied, "if you ever smelled his breath."

142

Two very drunk hillbillies were driving along a mountain road when suddenly they blew a tire, lost control of the car and went sailing over the cliff's edge.

As they plummeted downward, the hillbilly on the

passenger side screamed hysterically, "Oh, my God, Clem, we're gonna die!"

"Aw, don't worry about a thing," Clem reassured him, looking below. "There's a stop sign at the bottom."

143

The farmer was whitewashing the interior of his country outhouse and had the misfortune of falling through the opening. Standing knee-deep in shit, he hollered, "Fire! Fire! Fire!" at the top of his lungs. The local fire department responded to the alarm on the double, with tires squealing and sirens screaming as they skidded to a halt in front of the privy.

"Where's the fire?" called the chief.

"Ain't no fuckin' fire," replied the farmer as they hoisted him out of the two-holer, "but who the hell would've rescued me if I'd yelled, 'Shit! Shit! Shit!'?"

144

The HUSTLER Dictionary defines *adolescence* as: the stage of life between puberty and adultery.

145

A biker went to a shrink to find out why he was always feeling so depressed. The shrink, after questioning him about his job, family, childhood and hobbies, asked the man, "How long is it since you've had sex?"

The biker sat back and thought for a minute, then reached in his pocket and said, "It's still about eight inches . . . Why do you ask?"

146

Three middle-aged ladies were sitting on a park bench, discussing their husbands.

"My husband's like a sports car—fast and sleek," said the first one.

The second one remarked, "Mine's more like a Rolls-Royce—smooth, soft and polished."

The third looked up rather dejectedly and said, "Shit, my old man's like an old Model T—you gotta start him by hand, then jump on when he finally gets going!"

147

The old biker had taken to being courteous in his later years, especially to women. One day when airing his views, he remarked that he'd never seen an ugly female.

A woman standing near him with a very flat nose, waffled cheeks and no lips overheard this and said, "I beg your pardon, sir, but can you look at me and honestly say that I'm not ugly?"

The noble tramp gazed at her and replied, "My dear lady, like the rest of your sex, you are an angel fallen from the skies. It's not your fault that you happened to fall on your fuckin' face."

148

After twenty years of obedience to his vow of silence, a Trappist monk was called into the abbot's study and told that he could utter two words. "Bad food," he said softly. His superior nodded and dismissed him.

Twenty years later, the monk was called again by the abbot. "No heat," the monk said, head bowed.

By the time he was called again, a new, younger abbot had been appointed. The monk, an old man now, entered the study waving his cane. "I quit," he declared.

"So be it," the abbot said. "I hear you bitch too much anyway."

149

The Pope and a lawyer died at the same time and were standing at the gates of heaven.

Saint Peter said, "We've been expecting you two— your rooms are ready." Then he said to the lawyer, "Excuse me while I take the Pope to his room; I'll get right back to you and show you your own quarters."

"Hey, would you mind if I tagged along?" asked the lawyer.

"Not at all," said Saint Peter.

They arrived at the Pope's room. It had a twin bed, a single chair, a little table and a small radio.

It looked like an everyday motel room.

Saint Peter then took the lawyer to his room, and the attorney was shocked to see a huge suite with a spacious balcony, a king-size bed, a spiral staircase and a wide-screen color TV with remote control, stereo, VCR, the works.

"This room is terrific!" exclaimed the lawyer. "But why does the Pope have a dinky little room when I get this fabulous penthouse?"

"Well," said Saint Peter, "we've had many Popes up here, but you're the first lawyer to ever make it!"

150

After hearing that one of the patients in a mental hospital had saved another from a suicide attempt by pulling him out of a bathtub, the director reviewed the rescuer's file and called him into his office.

"Mr. Douglas, your records and your heroic behavior indicate that you're ready to go home," the director said. "I'm only sorry that the man you saved later committed suicide by hanging himself."

"Oh, he didn't hang himself," replied Douglas, "I hung him up to dry."

151

Sam had been a soldier of war for more than three years, during which he'd fought in many battles and had won numerous decorations. He was finally discharged from the service and returned home to his wife and son, whom he hadn't seen since he'd shipped out.

As Sam walked up the path to his house, his young son spotted him through the window and yelled, "Mom, here comes Daddy—and he's got a Purple Heart on!"

Rushing out of the kitchen, his mom promptly replied, "I don't give a damn what color it is—let him in right away, and you go play at the Joneses' for a couple of hours."

152

The HUSTLER Dictionary defines *bikini bottom* as: a gash mask.

153

Three friends from New York decided to get away from the summer heat by driving up to Canada to do some fishing. Having found a lake to their liking, the men launched their boat and headed out. After several hours, one of the men stood to reach for a beer, lost his balance and slid into the water. Twenty minutes later, his two friends noticed he was missing.

"Shit, Charley must have fallen in!" one exclaimed as he set his rod down and jumped in to search for his lost friend.

After a few dives, he dragged a soggy body up into the boat and immediately began performing mouth-to-mouth resuscitation.

"Jeez, I never knew Charley had such bad breath!" the rescuer said, coming up for air.

"Yeah," said the other, "and I don't remember Charley having on a snowmobile suit, either!"

154

Not long after his marriage, Bart and his father met for lunch. "Well, son," asked Mr. Wingo, "how is married life treating you?"

"Not very well, I'm afraid," sighed Bart. "It seems I married a nun."

"A nun?" his father asked.

"That's right," moaned Bart. "None in the morning, none at night and none at all unless I beg!"

The father nodded knowingly and slapped his boy on the back a couple of times. "Why don't we all get together for dinner tonight and have a nice talk?"

The young man smiled. "Say, Dad, that's a great idea!"

"Fine," replied the father, "I'll call home and tell the Mother Superior to set two extra plates."

155

Mr. Cockran stood on the bridge ready to jump. Just as he was about to, Father Bella came strolling by. "My son, please come down from there. Nothing is worth dying for."

"Oh, yeah?" asked Mr. Cockran. "Remember when my brother ran off with my wife?"

"Yes," replied the priest, "but that was over a year ago. Haven't you gotten over that yet?"

"Yes, I have," answered Mr. Cockran.

"Then why are you doing this?"

"Because he called this morning," sobbed Mr. Cockran, "and he's bringing her back!"

156

After much soul-searching and having determined the husband was infertile, the childless couple decided to try artificial insemination. When the woman showed up at the clinic, she was told to undress from the waist down, get on the table and place her feet in the stirrups. She was feeling rather awkward about the entire procedure when the doctor came in. Her anxiety was not diminished by the sight of him pulling down his pants.

"Wait a minute! What the hell is going on here?" yelped the woman, pulling herself into a sitting position.

"Don't you want to get pregnant?" asked the doctor.

"Well, yes, I do," answered the woman.

"Then lie back and spread 'em," replied the doctor. "We're all out of the bottled stuff—you'll just have to settle for what's on tap."

157

Two men were standing at adjacent urinals when one glanced over at the other and said, "I'll bet you were born in Newark, Ohio."

"Why, that's right!" said the second man in surprise.

"And I'll bet you were circumcised when you were three days old."

"Right again. But how did you—"

"And I'll bet it was done by old Doc Steadman."

"Well, yes," replied the astonished man, "but how on earth did you know?"

"Well, old Doc Steadman always cut them on a 60-degree angle," explained the first man, "and you're pissing on my shoe."

158

A couple was having a heated argument over money. "If it weren't for my money," the wife exploded, "this TV wouldn't be here! If it weren't for my money, that easy chair you're sitting in wouldn't be here! And if it weren't for my money, this house wouldn't be here!"

"Look, you stupid bitch," her husband snorted, "if it weren't for your money, I wouldn't be here!"

159

A crowd gathered on the yard at Folsom Prison, where a wild-eyed white man was jumping up and down on a manhole cover, energetically shouting, "Twenty-eight, twenty-eight!" Finally, one huge black guy was unable to restrain his curiosity. "What you doin' dat fo'?" he roughly questioned the jumper.

"It really relieves tension and cools you out—why don't you try it for yourself?" replied the white man.

So, somewhat reluctantly, the black man started jumping up and down on the manhole cover. Just as he was getting into a rhythm, the white guy pulled the cover out from under him, and the black man tumbled down into the hole.

Quickly replacing the cover, the white guy started jumping up and down again, joyfully shouting, "Twenty-nine, twenty-nine!"

160

Q: What do you get when you cross an agnostic, an insomniac and a dyslexic?

A: A guy who lies awake all night wondering if there really is a dog.

161

A prosecutor was working late in his office when the devil suddenly appeared and offered him a deal.

Beginning instantly, Satan said, the lawyer could win all his cases, become the most prominent prosecutor in the entire country, make three times as much money, work half as long, be idolized by his office workers, be taken care of by a beautiful, sex-starved secretary, marry the woman of his dreams and live a long, happy life. "All I want in exchange," the devil continued, "is your soul."

The attorney considered the offer. "So," he asked suspiciously, "what's the catch?"

162
Q: What would happen if Santa Claus were Jewish?
A: Presents would come C.O.D.

163
Learning that he had a rare disease for which the only cure was mother's milk, Mr. Grayson took out a personal ad to find a nursing woman. Much to his delight, a woman responded almost immediately. After agreeing on a price over the phone, he went to her apartment.

As it happened, Mr. Grayson had especially soft lips and an active tongue. After about five minutes of nursing, the woman was beside herself with passion. "Is there anything else I can offer you?" she huffed and puffed.

"If it's not too much trouble," answered Mr. Grayson, "do you happen to have any cookies?"

164

"I'm lonely," Adam complained to God in the Garden of Eden. "I need someone to keep me company."

"No problem," replied God. "I'm going to create a perfect mate for you, Adam. She will be beautiful, intelligent, gracious and loving. She'll be a great cook and a wonderful mother. She'll keep your home spotless, and she'll never talk back. How does that sound?"

"Sounds great!" said Adam. "But what's she gonna cost me?"

"An arm and a leg," God replied.

"Jeez, that's pretty steep, God," countered Adam. "What can I get for just a rib?"

165

The redneck farmer was disturbed when he found his son masturbating several times a day. "Boy, you got to stop that," he said. "Go out and get yourself a wife."

So the boy went out and soon found a pretty, young girl to whom he got married. But a week or so after the wedding, the farmer found his son whacking off again.

"You crazy boy!" the father yelled. "That Lucy Mae's a fine girl!"

"I know, Pop," the boy replied, "but her arm gets tired sometimes."

166

The Polack strutted into his office looking unusually sharp one morning. "How's it going, Bob?" asked one of his co-workers. "Hey—when did you get the new leather jacket and slacks?"

"They were a gift from the wife," Bob said smugly.

"No shit! Was it a surprise gift?"

"Yep," Bob replied. "I just walked into the bedroom last night, and there they were, hangin' over the chair."

167

Mike accompanied his wife when she went in for her annual checkup. Afterward, while she was getting dressed, the doc came out of the examining room and said, "Frankly, I don't like the way she looks."

"Shit, neither do I," said Mike, "but she's handy around the house."

168

Q: When does a Mexican become a Spaniard?

A: When he marries into your family.

169

On the advice of a marriage counselor, Bob and Sue rented a lakeside cabin for a weekend together.

When they returned on Monday, Sue's best friend asked her, "So how did you and your ol' man get along over the weekend?"

"Pretty good. Every morning he took me out to the middle of the lake in the rowboat and let me swim back."

"Jeez, hon, wasn't that kinda far to swim?"

"It wasn't too bad," replied Sue. "The really hard part was getting out of the bag first."

170

While out with his friends barhopping one night, Mark was asked why he always sent his ex-wife her alimony payment fifteen days early. Mark shuddered and explained, "I'm afraid that if I'm ever late with the payment, she might decide to repossess me!"

171

A sodbuster in Missouri called up the sheriff and informed him that he'd just run over three lawyers and that the sheriff could come see about them if he wanted to. When the sheriff showed up about three hours later, he asked the sodbuster where the lawyers were.

"I thought you wouldn't want to bother with 'em," he said. "So I just went ahead and buried 'em."

"You buried 'em?" asked the sheriff. "Are you sure they was all dead?"

"Well," the sodbuster said, "they said they wasn't, but you know how those lawyers lie."

172

A hick from a small town was forced to take a blood test to determine if he was the father of a local teenage girl's baby. He was scared shitless before taking the test, but when he left the lab he was all smiles.

"Well," asked one of his buddies, "can they prove you're the father?"

"No fucking way!" gloated the hick. "That dumb-ass lab technician took the samples from my finger!"

173

Q: What do you call two black highway patrolmen?
A: Chocolate chips.

174

Two Arab terrorists were driving through the streets of Jerusalem when one turned to the other and nervously asked, "Abdul, what if the bomb in the backseat blows up before we get there?"

Abdul smiled and said, "Hey, don't worry about it— I've got another one in the trunk!"

175

The young Irish bride made her first appointment with a gynecologist and told him of her and her husband's wish to start a family. "We've been trying for months now, and I don't seem to be able to get pregnant," she confessed miserably.

"I'm sure we'll solve the problem," the doctor reassured her. "If you'll just get up on the examination table and take off your underpants . . ."

"Well, all right, Doctor," agreed the blushing young woman, "but I'd rather have my husband's baby."

176

Two men were having a drink when one asked, "I heard you and your wife split up. What happened?"

"Hey," he answered, "would you put up with someone having wild parties, coming home at all hours of the night and having friends over to stay as long as they liked?"

"Nope," the first said, "can't say I would."

"Neither would my wife, so I left."

177

One day while out shooting grub, a backwoods hillbilly found a mirror which had been lost by a backpacker.

"Well, if it ain't my Pa," he mumbled to himself as he picked it up and gazed into it. "I never knew Pa had his picture took."

Taking the mirror home, he stashed it away in the attic, but his actions got his wife suspicious. That night she slipped up to the attic and found the mirror. "So this is the old hag he's been slippin' off to see!"

178

Ben and Doug were out deep-sea fishing when their boat struck a reef and sank like a rock.

To make matters worse, as they started to swim for an island in the distance, a shark attacked Doug, mauling both his arms and legs. Ben swam back for him and said, "The island's not far off now, pal. Climb on my back, and I'll dog paddle us both to shore."

Finally reaching the island, Ben hauled his partner out of the water and onto the beach, where they both collapsed.

"Holy shit," Ben said, exhausted. "I'm fucked!"

"Sorry, Ben," Doug said sheepishly, "but it was the only way I could hold on."

179

Q: What's the difference between a Jewish American Princess and a Mexican American Princess?

A: With a Mexican American Princess, the jewelry is fake and the orgasms are real.

180

Two Polish citizens walked into a brand-new post office in Warsaw, and the first thing that caught their eye was a bunch of "Wanted" posters, in particular a shot of one mean-looking Russian beneath a banner that read: WANTED—SERIAL RAPIST.

"You know," said one Pole to the other, "that really pisses me off. They still get the best jobs!"

181

Joe waited outside while his friend Henry went into his house for a minute to tell his wife he was going to play poker with the boys.

An hour later, Joe stepped up to the screen door and yelled in, "Hey, Henry! Just how much longer are you going to be?"

"Not long," Henry hollered back. "It's almost my turn to talk."

182

Bob was kicking back in his living room one afternoon when there came a loud pounding at the front door, and on the stoop stood two men in blue. Waving a search warrant in his face, the first cop said, "We're going to search your house, you fucking asshole, and this warrant gives us the right. We're also going to search your front and back yards, and there's not a damn thing you can do about it!"

"Go ahead," Bob said as he went back to the living room to sit down.

After the cops tore up the house, they headed for the backyard. Immediately, Bob heard the cops screaming bloody murder. Bob got up and looked out the window to see the pair racing like hell around the yard, with three pit bulls right on their asses.

"Call 'em off! Call 'em off!" screamed the cops.

"Fuck you, assholes!" Bob yelled. "Show them your fucking warrant!"

183

Q: Why do women have bellybuttons?
A: So men will have a handy place to keep the tartar sauce.

184

Jim went to the doctor, complaining that his wife was very sick.

"Your wife has been coming in here every week for two years with different complaints," the doctor said. "There's nothing wrong with her. She just thinks she's sick."

The next morning, Jim was back at the clinic.

"How's your wife now?" asked the doctor.

"She thinks she'd dead," came the reply.

185

Mike and Bill were the best of friends and shared an apartment together. One day Mike came home to find Bill weeping into his hands. "I can't take any more. I'm the unluckiest person in the world!"

"You're always saying that, and it's just not true," replied Mike. "What's happened now?"

"Well, I met this beautiful woman on the street. We got to talking, and we stopped off at a bar. Then she suggested we go to her place, and I thought my luck had changed. Minutes after we entered her apartment, we were in the sack. I was just about to climax when we heard the front door slam and her husband call out. I didn't even have time to grab a towel. I leaped out the window and was hanging onto the ledge with my hands when he barged in, looked around and saw my hands."

"Jesus!" Mike exclaimed. "What happened then?"

"Terrible things," replied Bill. "He came over to the window and started banging on my knuckles with a hammer. Then he whipped out his dick and pissed all over me. Then he slammed the window down on my hands. Then, just to make matters worse, two old ladies saw me hanging there stark naked and called the cops, and they arrested me. Now do you see why I say I'm so unlucky?"

"Nonsense," Mike responded. "That could have happened to anyone."

"You don't understand," countered Bill. "When the cops arrested me, I looked down at my feet, and they were only four inches off the ground!"

186

Q: Did you hear about the Polish airliner that crashed into a graveyard?

A: So far, they've recovered 7,000 bodies.

187

While trying to persuade his new girlfriend to come over, the young man had finally led the phone conversation in a romantic direction.

"Yes, I do like a dry white wine," she said.

"Great. I have two bottles chilling now."

"And I just love Janet Jackson."

"Just got her new CD."

"My fantasy is making love on a fur rug in front of a fireplace."

"No problem," he said instantly. "I'll shoot the dog."

188

"You're in excellent shape, Mrs. DiMaggio," pronounced the doctor with a smile at the conclusion of her annual physical. "Is there anything else I could help you with?"

Mrs. DiMaggio nodded, then blushed. "You know how Sam is about doctors; he'd never ask you about this, Dr. Jones, but he's been having trouble with impotence. Is there any medication that could help him?"

"Of course," said the doctor. He then wrote out a prescription, which Mrs. DiMaggio filled on the way home. Unfortunately, the pharmacist made a mistake typing the label, writing three tablespoons instead of three teaspoons as the daily dosage.

When Dr. Jones got to his office the next morning, his phone was ringing off the hook. It was a frantic Mrs. DiMaggio.

"What's wrong?" asked the doctor. "Didn't the medicine work?"

"I'll say it did!" she cried. "He's jumped every woman on the block, and now he's chasing a cat down the street!"

189

The HUSTLER Dictionary defines *coin-operated robot hookers* as: slut machines.

190

After spending a vigorous night with a hooker, the senator took $300 out of his wallet and set it on the motel nightstand.

"Thanks, but I only charge $20," the woman said.

"Twenty dollars for the entire night?" the incredulous politician asked. "You can't possibly make a living on that!"

"Oh, don't worry," she purred. "I do a little blackmailing on the side."

191

Q: Did you hear about the hillbilly who left his estate in trust for his wife?

A: She can't touch it until she's 13.

192

The minister was sick, and a pastor noted for his long-winded sermons agreed to fill in. When he stood up in the pulpit, he found only four churchgoers present.

Afterward, he complained to the sexton. "That was the smallest turnout I've ever seen," he said. "Weren't they informed that I was coming?"

"Nope," replied the sexton, "but somehow word must've leaked out."

193

A traveling salesman completed his trip earlier than anticipated and sent his wife a telegram: "Returning home Friday."

Arriving home, he found his wife in bed with another man. Being a nonviolent person and a major wimp, he bitterly complained to his father-in-law, who replied, "Don't get so upset. I'm certain that there must be an explanation."

The next day the father-in-law was all smiles. "I knew there was an explanation," he informed his son-in-law. "She didn't get your telegram!"

194

A worried husband told the marriage counselor, "I'm afraid I'm losing my wife's love."

The counselor asked, "Has she started to neglect you?"

The husband said, "No, she's as attentive as ever.

She meets me at the door with a cold drink and a warm kiss. My shirts are always ironed. She cooks the foods I like, she keeps the house neat and clean, she makes the kids stay out of my hair, and she even lets me choose the TV programs we watch. Our sex life is still as good as ever, and she never objects to kinky stuff or says she has a headache."

"Then what *do* you think is wrong?" exclaimed the counselor.

His patient replied, "Well, maybe I'm just being overly sensitive. But at night, when she thinks I'm sleeping, she puts her lips up close to my ear and whispers, *'Die! Die! You son of a bitch!'* "

195

The HUSTLER Dictionary defines *Mexican Superman* as: a guy who can steal the tires off flying airplanes.

196

Finishing his prepared statement, the blustering politician threw his press conference open for questions.

"Is it true that you were born in a log cabin?" one sarcastic reporter asked.

"You're thinking of Abraham Lincoln," the politician answered. "I was born in a manger."

197

After his wife died, the biker met with a funeral director. "What would you like to say in the obituary?"
asked the director.

" 'Sandy died,' " said the biker.

"That's too short. You should have at least five
words."

"All right," replied the biker. "How about, 'Sandy
died. Cadillac for sale.' "

198

Q: Why is it that California has the most lawyers and
New Jersey has the most toxic-waste dumps?

A: New Jersey had first choice.

199

A famous Russian ballerina defected to the U.S., and
there was considerable excitement on the night of her
American premiere. Everything went along smoothly
before a very receptive audience. Finally it was time for
the grand finale. The entire troupe swirled about the
ballerina, who performed a spectacular set of leaps and
landed in a perfect split at center stage.

Needless to say, the crowd went wild. It was only
after a standing ovation and five curtain calls that the

curtain closed for the last time. Rushing onstage to the ballerina, who was still holding the perfect split, the director began to congratulate her on her superb performance.

"Performance, hell," hissed the dancer. "Rock me back and forth to break the seal."

200

The stud was hanging out at his house one day when the phone rang.

"Hi, this is Cindy," the voice said. "Remember me?"

The promiscuous guy had met too many Cindys in his life. "Uh, no, sorry . . . I can't place you at the moment."

"You took me home after Jane's Christmas party, remember? You said I was a good sport."

"Oh, yeah, now I remember you. How you doin'?"

"Not so good," she answered. "I just found out I'm pregnant, and I want to kill myself."

Without missing a beat, the slick guy answered, "Hey—I was right! You really are a good sport."

201

Q: How bad is the AIDS epidemic?
A: Well, it's now safer to skip the sex and go right to the cigarette.

202

Thoroughly fed up with his wife's incessant bitching and moaning, Joe finally agreed to accompany her to a meeting with her therapist. Once there, he made his reluctance quite clear; explaining that he had absolutely no idea how she found so much to complain about all the time.

"Well, Mr. Smith," the therapist pointed out gently, "it is customary for married people to have sexual intercourse regularly, even frequently. Mrs. Smith tells me that even on the nights when you don't fall asleep in front of the TV, you never respond in any way to her sexual advances."

"Yeah, well, so?" Joe scratched his head. "So whaddaya recommend?"

"Well, a reasonable minimum might be sexual intercourse at least twice a week," suggested the counselor.

"Twice a week, huh?" grunted Joe, thinking it over. "Okay, I could drop her off on Mondays . . . but on Fridays she's got to take the bus."

203

God looked down from Heaven one day and saw a man exercising. The guy was counting off as he worked out. God was in a playful mood that day and decided to do a little experimenting. First He took out the left side of the brain. The man counted, "One, three, five . . ." After

He put the left side back, He took out the right. Now the man counted, "Two, four, six . . ."

Suddenly God got a mischievous urge and decided to take out both sides of the guy's brain. Now the guy counted off, *"Uno, dos, tres . . ."*

204

Henry had been a staunch Republican all his life. At 95 years old, his health was failing fast. One morning, he asked his son to take him to the courthouse downtown so he could change his registration from Republican to Democrat.

"But, Dad," protested the young man, "you started this town's Republican party. Why would you want to become a Democrat?"

"Son," replied Henry, "if someone has to die, it might as well be one of them."

205

"He's great on the court," a sportswriter said of a college basketball player in an interview with the coach, "but how's his scholastic record?"

"Why, he makes straight A's," replied the coach.

"That's great!" said the sportswriter.

"Yes," agreed the coach, "but his fucking B's are still a little crooked."

206

Q: What's the difference between a Harley and a
   Hoover?

A: The position of the dirt bag.

207

Three friends were walking around town when they
came across a prostitute soliciting on a street corner.
Attracted to her good looks, they inquired about her
rate. "Actually, I operate on a sliding scale," said the
girl. "You see, I charge $10 an inch."

The men accepted and went off to her apartment.
They took turns with her. The first man told his friends
proudly that he had paid $70. The second guy an-
nounced that he had not received any change from a
$100 bill. The third man declared that it was by far the
best time he had ever had for $20. The other two stared
at their feet and began to snicker uncontrollably.

"I don't know what you two fools find so funny,"
said the third man. "Neither of you had the sense to pay
on the way out . . ."

208

"We rarely, if ever, use the word *cure*," said the psychiatrist to his patient. "But after six years of intense therapy, it is my pleasure to pronounce you completely
cured."

To the shrink's surprise, an unhappy look came over the woman's face.

"What's wrong?" he asked. "I thought you'd be thrilled."

"Oh, it's fine for you," she explained. "But try to look at it from my point of view. Six years ago, I was Joan of Arc. Now, I'm nobody."

209

"Come on, Frank," one friend said to another, "your wife's not as bad as you make her out to be. What would you do if you found her in bed with another man?"

"I'd break his cane and shoot his dog!"

210

Francine died and went to heaven, where she was given a tour of the place by the angel Dionne, who wanted to make sure the new arrival felt at home. "We have all kinds," the angel explained, pointing out a group of Moslems drinking Turkish coffee in one corner, a number of Buddhists gathered under a tree, and a group of rabbis strolling by, making sure their yarmulkes didn't fly away in the breeze.

A high wall to one side couldn't obscure the tinkle of

piano music, the clinking of ice in glasses and the dull roar of pleasant conversation. "And who's behind the wall?" inquired Francine.

"Shh," cautioned Angel Dionne. "Those are the Catholics. They like to think they're the only one's here."

211

Q: What's the difference between love, true love and showing off?

A: Spitting, swallowing and gargling.

212

The aging mother was on her deathbed, and one of her last wishes was to find out what was happening with her youngest son, Charlie. Charlie had been a very strange, sick child who had run away from home at age 16. One of her daughters agreed to track Charlie down, and the old woman clung to life. Finally, the daughter returned and told her mother. "I found Charlie, and I've got some good news and some bad news."

The mother whispered, "What's the good news?"

"He's off drugs, and he spends all of his time stuffing animals."

"And what's the bad news?"

"He's not a taxidermist."

213

A busy surgeon returned from a two-week hunting trip complaining angrily to his wife, "I didn't kill a damn thing!"

"Well, darling," she replied, "that's what you get for neglecting your practice."

214

The HUSTLER Dictionary defines *masturbation* as: a self-service elevator.

215

Stella had a question for her husband, Stewart, on their wedding night.

"How will I let you know," she asked, "when I want to have sex?"

"On the nights you want sex, reach over and tug my dick," Stewart told her. "On the nights you don't want sex, reach over and tug it about 350 times."

216

The HUSTLER Dictionary defines *condom* as: a cock smock.

217

Rick saw a small boy on the street smoking a cigarette.

"Such a young boy to have such a bad habit," Rick scolded. "How old are you, son?"

"Six," the tyke answered.

"How long have you been smoking?" Rick asked.

"Ever since the first night I had sex with a girl."

Rick was dumbfounded. "How long ago was that?" he inquired.

"I can't remember," the boy said. "I was quite drunk at the time."

218

Q: What did the cannibal do after he dumped his girl-friend?

A: He wiped.

219

"Oh, doctor," the homosexual wept upon being diagnosed with AIDS. "Is there any treatment you can give me?"

"I think you should go to Mexico and live it up," the MD advised. "Drink all the water you can. Have plenty of tequila too. Also be sure to consume as much Mexican cuisine as possible—especially raw fruits and vegetables."

"Will that cure me?" the gay man asked.

"No," the doc said, "but it will teach you what your asshole is for."

220

Three expectant fathers waited in the maternity ward: an Italian, a Chinaman and a Jew. In waltzed the nurse with a newborn black baby in her arms.

"Is this baby yours?" she asked the Italian.

"I don't think so," he replied.

"Is he yours?" she asked the Chinaman.

"It doesn't seem likely," he answered.

Finally she turned to the Jew. "Could this baby belong to you?"

"Probably," he answered. "My wife burns everything."

221

Q: Why did God give women foreheads?
A: So you have someplace to kiss them after they give you a blowjob.

222

Q: How can you tell the Irishman in a hospital ward?
A: He's the one blowing foam off the bedpans.

223

The HUSTLER Dictionary defines *mine shaft* as: a proud German's penis.

224

Hank had been invited for dinner to meet his girlfriend's parents. As the meal was being served, he felt a powerful fart welling up. He held on for as long as possible, but eventually let forth a loud ass-flapper. Thinking fast, Hank glared down at the family dog, who was lying under the table.

"Fido," his girlfriend's mother warned, "behave yourself!"

A few minutes later, Hank cut loose yet another ripe butt blast.

Again, the matriarch cautioned her dog: *"Fido!"*

After dessert, Hank fired forth his worst gas attack of the evening.

"That's it, Fido!" the mother declared. "Come out from under there, before Hank shits all over you!"

225

Q: What do you call a Spanish homosexual?
A: A señor-eater.

226

A couple of nuns were walking into town on convent business. Suddenly a stranger leapt from the bushes, tackled one of the sisters and savagely raped her.

Following her brutal attack, the victimized bride of Christ turned to her companion and said, "This is terrible! How will I explain to Mother Superior that I was raped twice in one night?"

"Twice?" her puzzled friend asked.

"Well, we *are* coming back this way, aren't we?"

227

Q: What's the difference between an Irish wedding and an Irish funeral?

A: There's one less drunk at the funeral.

228

Examining the license of a hot young girl he'd pulled over, the motorcycle cop asked, "Is this a Polish name?"

"Yes," the suspect replied. Promptly thereafter, the officer unzipped his fly.

"Oh, no," the Polish princess cried out. "Not another breathalyzer test!"

229

Tony walked into a bar and took note of two unusual sights: a horse serving the drinks, and a jar filled with $5 bills.

Tony ordered a beer from the equine bartender and turned to the guy seated next to him.

"What's up with the jar of 5s?" he asked.

"It's a contest," his neighbor explained. "You put a 5 in the jar, and if you can make the horse laugh, you get to keep all the others."

Tony felt confident. He deposited his entry fee and summoned the horse into the men's room. When they returned, the horse was convulsed with laughter. Tony collected his jackpot.

Several months later, he returned to the same bar. This time the contest jar was filled with $10 bills. Tony asked the patron he'd met last time if the rules had changed.

"Now you have to make the horse cry," the regular answered.

With that, Tony dropped his 10 in the till and called the horse into the john again. When they returned to the barroom, the horse was crying hysterically.

"I've got to know," Tony's buddy urged him. "How did you do that?"

"The first time, I told him I was hung better than he was," explained Tony. "This time, I showed him."

230

The HUSTLER Dictionary defines *chocolate-covered cherries* as: African-American virgins.

231

As Jimmy walked alongside his father, he noticed a pair of dogs getting it on.

"What are they doing?" the boy asked.

"Making a puppy," his father responded.

Later that night, Jimmy passed his parents' bedroom and caught them in the middle of sex.

"Hey, Pop," he called. "What's going on now?"

"Well, we're making you a baby brother," his father answered.

"Well, flip her around then," said Jimmy. "I'd rather have a puppy."

232

Q: What are two fingers to a bulimic?
A: Dessert.

233

The HUSTLER Dictionary defines *rib-tickler* as: a vibrator shoved in way too deep.

234

Q: What do you call a leper in a hot tub?

A: Stew.

235

"Eureka!" Professor Vrusho exclaimed. "I've invented an apple that tastes like pussy!"

With great enthusiasm, he offered his colleague Dr. Verilla a sample.

Verilla took one bite and spit it out in disgust. "This apple tastes like shit!" he hollered.

"Indeed," said Professor Vrusho, beaming. "Turn it around."

236

The HUSTLER Dictionary defines *cocktail party* as: an affair where a man gets stiff, a woman gets tight, and they return home to find that neither is either.

237

Dave rushed to his urologist in great pain.

"Doctor," he explained, "my entire genital area is red, itchy and inflamed."

Examining him, the medic asked, "Do you have sex with your wife often?"

"Twice a day," Dave answered, "and three times on weekends."

"What about girlfriends?" the doc inquired.

"I have two," Dave confessed, "and I have sex with them all the time."

"Well, I think your problems are connected to all that intensive sexual contact."

"Oh, splendid! I thought it was because I masturbated too much!"

238

Q: How do you use a condom twice?

A: You turn it inside out and shake the fuck out of it.

239

Two young boys tore all over town in a go-cart that was being pulled by a dog. A policeman eventually stopped them and ruined their fun.

"Boys, this is very cruel," he said, cutting the rope that was tied around the dog's neck. He then noticed a second cord wrapped around the mutt's testicles. "My goodness!" the officer exclaimed. "It's worse than I thought!"

"Shit!" the boy in front said to his pal. "There goes our overdrive!"

240

A Russian, a Jamaican, an American and a Mexican found themselves on a rafting expedition. As they paddled downriver, the Russian opened a bottle of vodka, took one gulp and tossed the rest overboard.

"What did you do that for?" the stunned American asked.

"In my country," the Russian explained, "vodka is so plentiful, we can afford to waste it."

A bit later, the Jamaican lit up a huge joint, took a few puffs on the marijuana and then tossed it over the side.

"Hey," the American exclaimed. "that stuff is expensive."

"Ganja grows so abundantly in my country," the Jamaican told him, "we can afford to waste it."

The American sat back and thought hard for a moment. Then he stood up and threw the Mexican into the river.

241

The HUSTLER Dictionary defines *protein* as: a hooker under the age of 20.

242

Sam was feeling horny one night, so he reached over to his wife, Doris.

"Not tonight," Doris said. "I have a gynecologist's appointment in the morning. I'm not supposed to have sex for twenty-four hours before I get there."

Thinking fast, Sam patted Doris on the back of the head and said, "Ah, but you don't have a dentist's appointment tomorrow, do you?"

243

"I'll never forget the first time I turned to alcohol as a substitute for women," said one Bowery bum to the other.

"Really?" his pal asked. "What happened?"

"It took me half the night to get my dick unstuck from the neck of the bottle."

244

The day of her scheduled procedure, Mary waited in the abortion clinic. Next to her, a woman sat calmly working with yarn and knitting needles.

"Excuse me," Mary asked, "but isn't it kind of sick for you to be knitting baby booties right before you have an abortion?"

"Oh, I'm not making booties," the woman answered. "It's a body bag."

245

Q: Why don't Jews drink?

A: It interferes with their suffering.

246

Stewart, a supermarket bag boy, carried a divorcee's bundles into the parking lot.

Eyeing her hunky helper, the horny woman purred, "I've got an itchy pussy."

"Well, you better point it out," Stewart responded. "All those Japanese cars look alike to me."

247

Q: How many mice does it take to screw in a light-bulb?

A: Just two. The problem is getting them in the light-bulb.

248

Lying in bed with his wife, a farmer reached over and stroked her bare breasts. "You know, Maybelle," he said, "if these gave milk, we could sell the cow."

Sighing, Maybelle patted her husband's crotch. "And if this stayed hard longer," she said, "we could fire the farmhand."

249

A lawyer and a Catholic priest found themselves with two children in front of the last lifeboat on a rapidly sinking ship.

"There's room for only two of us," the lawyer said to the priest. "Let's you and me take it. Screw the kids!"

Perplexed, the clergyman asked, "Do you think we'll have time before the ship goes down?"

250

Doris asked the pharmacist: "Do you have condoms in size extra-extra-large?"

"Yes," he responded. "Do you want some?"

"No, thanks," Doris said. "But would you mind if I hung around until someone comes in who does?"

251

Q: What do you get when you cross a blank and an Indian?

A: A Sioux named Boy.

252

Ted brought a hooker to his hotel room. "I want to try something *really* different," he said.

"Okay," she told him. "We'll do sixty-nine."

The hooker lowered her snatch toward Ted's lips. Suddenly, she let loose a loud, stinking fart.

Ted jumped and ran for the door.

"What's the matter?" the hooker called after him.

"No way can I stand sixty-eight more of those," he replied.

253

Q: What goes clip-clop, clip-clop, BANG, clip-clop, clip-clop?
A: An Amish drive-by shooting.

254

The HUSTLER Dictionary defines *wedding* as: a funeral where you smell your own flowers.

255

Timmy loved his new toy train set. It was big enough for him to ride around on, which he did all day long, repeatedly announcing, "All the motherfuckers gettin' on, get on! All the motherfuckers gettin' off, get off!"

Shocked to hear such language coming from her 8-year-old son, Timmy's mother sent him to his room.

"Don't come out," she warned, "until you've cleaned up your act."

After Timmy sulked away most of the afternoon, his mother saw how much he missed the train, so at last she relented and told him to go play.

The boy raced gleefully to the model engine and, hopping aboard, declared: "We are back in service, motherfuckers, and if any of you assholes has got shit to say about the three hour delay, take it to the bitch in the kitchen!"

256

Richardson rushed to the doctor, astonished to see that his dick had turned bright orange overnight.

"Perhaps your behavior brought on this condition," the medic proposed. "What were you doing the last time you remember your penis being its normal color?"

"I was taking it easy," Richardson replied. "My new *Hustler* had just come in the mail; so I sat down to enjoy it with a big bag of Cheetos."

257

Q: Why are schizophrenics afraid to shave?
A: They don't trust that fucker with the razor.

258

A pair of young girls from the mountains rode down to a nearby village on their bikes.

"I've never come this way before," observed one.

"Neither have I," said the other. "It must be the cobblestones."

259

One brutally humid day in ancient Egypt, a galley filled with slaves was rowing Cleopatra's barge up the Nile.

The captain approached them with good news and bad news. "The good news," he shouted, "is that you will all have the rest of the morning off. You may do whatever you wish for a few hours, and then meet in the royal dining cabin for a feast at midday."

"What's the bad news?" one of the slaves called out.

"This afternoon," the captain answered, "the Queen wants to go water-skiing."

260

The HUSTLER Dictionary defines *swap meat* as: two fags in a sixty-nine.

261

Looking upon his wife's bare, open pussy on the night of their golden anniversary, Chet wept uncontrollably.

"What's wrong?" his spouse queried.

"Fifty years ago, I couldn't wait to eat it," Chet dourly responded, "and now it looks like it can't wait to eat me!"

262

Three pals sat in a bar discussing their children.

"I've got five boys," boasted Ross, "enough for a basketball team."

"Well, I've got nine boys," trumpeted Johnson, "enough for a baseball team."

Clark, the third man, smiled broadly. "I've got eighteen girls," he beamed, "enough for a golf course."

263

Walter the Magnificent was finally booked on a major television variety show. The act was amazing. From his pocket, Walter took out a tiny, perfectly formed human being, dressed in a tuxedo, who sat at a miniature grand piano and played Beethoven's *Moonlight* Sonata.

The audience went wild over the act, and the host asked Walter where he found the little man.

"I was in an antique store," he said, "and I came across an old lamp. I brought it home and started to polish it, and suddenly a genie popped out and granted me a wish."

"And you asked for a twelve-inch *pianist*?"

"Not exactly."

264

A biker and his ol' lady were parked beside the road, watching a movie scene being filmed. The director suddenly got an idea for a fight scene. He said to the leading man, "You see that biker and his girl over there? Go over and insult her. Then, when the dude starts fighting with you, we'll get some real action shots."

The husky actor walked over to the biker and asked, "Is that cunt your ol' lady?"

"Fuckin' right!" the biker exclaimed.

"Well," the actor said, "she's the ugliest bitch I've ever seen."

The biker turned to his ol' lady and said, "See? What'd I tell you?"

265

An amorous couple was traveling down a country road. The girl stripped in the front seat, pulled out her lover's cock and began to give him head. He enjoyed it immensely—so much so, in fact, that he closed his eyes and lost control of the speeding car.

There was a horrible crash, pinning the man under the wheel but throwing the girl clear. In a panic she snatched up one of her boyfriends's shoes to cover her cunt and ran off down the road for help. She came upon a farmer plowing his field. Running up to him, she screamed, "Please, please you've got to help us! My boyfriend's stuck!"

The farmer glanced at the shoe covering the girl's crotch and said, "Ma'am, if he's in that far, there's not much I can do for him."

266

Q: Why shouldn't you screw your wife first thing in the morning?

A: You've got all day to find something better.

267

When his new patient was settled comfortably on the couch, the psychiatrist began his therapy session. "I'm not aware of your problem," the doctor said, "so let's start at the beginning."

"Yes, that's a good idea," the man said. "In the beginning, I created the heaven and the earth . . ."

268

The HUSTLER Dictionary defines *R.S.V.P.* as: Jewish slang for "Remember, send vedding present."

269

A Marine, an Air Force commando, a Navy Seal and a Green Beret were sitting around a campfire, telling each other how mean and tough they were.

"I can swim fifty miles and bite the head off a live chicken," the Marine said. "One Marine is worth *ten* other men!"

"I can jump out of airplanes without a parachute and clear runways single-handed!" the Air Force commando exclaimed. "One of us is worth *thirteen* other men!"

"I can dive ninety feet underwater without scuba gear, and I'm an expert in demolition," boasted the Navy man. "One Seal is worth *twenty-five* of the enemy!"

The Green Beret just sat there all this time without saying a word, stirring the fire with his dick.

270

An escaped convict broke into a house and tied up a young couple who had been sleeping in the bedroom.

As soon as he had a chance, the husband turned to his voluptuous young wife, bound up on the bed in a skimpy nightgown, and whispered, "Honey, this guy hasn't seen a woman in years. Just cooperate with anything he wants. If he wants to have sex with you, just go along with it and pretend you like it. Our lives depend on it."

"Dear," the wife hissed, spitting out her gag. "I'm so relieved you feel that way, because he just told me he thinks you have a really nice, tight-looking ass."

271

Q: What do you get when you combine fifty lesbians and fifty government workers?
A: One hundred people who don't do dick.

272

An ocean liner got shipwrecked a half mile from shore in shark-infested waters.

The ship's captain ran to the deck and shouted, "If anyone can swim past those sharks, it's me! I've had twenty years' experience in these waters!" With that, he jumped in and was immediately torn to pieces by a dozen frenzied sharks.

A minister ran up, beseeching the heavens: "Lord, I pray, protect me from those sharks so that I might save the lives of all souls on board!" The minister dove into the waters and was eaten in three gulps by a great white shark.

When a lawyer kicked off his wing tip shoes and

plunged into the water, the sharks parted and cleared a path for him to swim all the way to shore.

As soon as the lawyer reached help on shore, an amazed rescuer looked out at the shark-filled waters and shouted, "Nobody could have made it through that treacherous sea! It's a miracle!"

"Miracle, my ass," the lawyer scoffed, looking out at the sharks, "that was professional courtesy."

273

Mary asked her husband, Ralph, to fix the TV set. He gave her his usual answer. "Hell, no. What do I look like, a fucking TV repairman?"

That night, the toilet started to run. "Will you fix it, dear?" Mary asked.

"Hell no. What do I look like, a fucking plumber?"

The next day, when Ralph came home from work, he saw Mary with a big grin on her face and all the appliances in the house working like new.

"Good, you finally got the repairmen to come out."

"No," Mary replied, "it was Willy from next door. He told me he'd fix everything for free if I either baked him a pie or had sex with him."

Ralph shot her a suspicious glance. "You did bake him a pie, didn't you?"

Mary smiled. "Hell, no. What do I look like, a fucking pastry chef?"

274

A young puppy ran up to his father and yelped, "I just saw something really gross. Two humans were sticking their tongues into each other's mouth."

"I know it seems disgusting, son," his father growled authoritatively while licking his balls, "but that's just their way of sniffing butts."

275

Q: Why did Maria Shriver marry Arnold Schwartzenegger?

A: They're trying to breed a bullet-proof Kennedy.

276

The cops arrested a guy at the local mortuary who was screwing a dead brunette.

"Why, you sick little fuck," one of the cops taunted him. "Why the hell can't you have sex with live women like everybody else?"

"I used to," the suspect pleaded, "but every time I did, they called the cops on me."

277

An Aztec warrior entered the sleeping chamber of a beautiful maiden. "Bad news," the warrior announced,

"I just found out that you're going to be killed tomorrow in the sacrifice of the virgin."

"What will I do?" the virgin screamed.

"Relax," the warrior said, pulling out his dick and letting it grow hard in this hand. "Spread your legs, and I'll start saving your life immediately."

278

A Mexican, a black guy and a Polack were walking down the street when a crazed junkie approached, waving a blood-encrusted syringe at them.

"This needle's infected with AIDS," the junkie shouted. "Give me your money, or I'll jab you with it!"

"Anything you want, amigo," the Mexican said, handing over his wallet.

"It's all yours, brother. Take it," the black man insisted, hurriedly passing his wallet over to the junkie.

"Not on your life," the Polack spoke up, defiantly crossing his arms. "You can't have it!"

The junkie lunged, stuck the needle into the Polack's arm and ran off.

"What the hell did you do?" the black guy and the Mexican shouted. "He might have given you AIDS!"

"It's okay," the Polack replied confidently. "I'm wearing a condom."

279

After sleeping with a rancid street whore, Jake con-
tracted so many sexually transmitted diseases, his
doctors told him there was only one cure: immediate
surgery to remove his penis.

Desperate for a less radical solution, Jake consulted
an old Chinese herbalist. "I know problem," the ancient
Chinese medicine man muttered after examining
Jake's sore-covered penis. "You sleep with prostitute,
get much sick and go to American doctor. Problem
with American doctor, he always think surgery first.
He does not consider the natural way of the body and
spirit."

"You mean," Jake asked, brightening, "my dick
doesn't have to be surgically removed?"

"No surgery," the wise man from the East declared.
"You go home, take medicine tea I give you, wait two,
maybe three week, and pecker fall off all by itself."

280

The HUSTLER Dictionary defines *divorced female* as: a
woman without an asshole.

281

A man went into a bar with ten bucks and asked the
bartender if it was enough to get him laid.

"No problem," the bartender replied, taking the man's money. "There's a girl downstairs on the pool table who'll take care of your every need."

The man went downstairs and had a wild time with the girl on the pool table. When it was over, he noticed large quantities of white fluid dribbling out of her snatch. Too nervous to say anything to the girl about it, he ran upstairs and mentioned the unusual milky discharge to the bartender.

"I'm sorry about that, sir," the bartender apologized. "We'll take care of it right away."

The bartender turned to a busboy cleaning off a table. "Pedro, I've got a job for you. Go empty out the dead one. She's full again."

282

After sleeping with a geisha girl on his business trip to Japan, Bob asked her why she had kept shouting *"ya-mashika!"* throughout their lovemaking session.

"Because," explained the polite geisha girl, *"ya-mashika* means 'you are so good!' "

The next day when his Japanese business associate hit a hole in one on the golf course, Bob shouted, *"Yamashika!"*

"Yamashika?" his Japanese business associate asked, totally confused. "What do you mean, 'wrong hole'?"

283

Muggsy's first stop after being released from jail was a nearby whorehouse. "I need to eat some pussy," he told the woman at the desk. "Right away."

"Well, you might have to wait," she answered. "There's been some trouble, and I don't know if anyone's avail—"

"I need to eat some pussy now!" Muggsy roared. "Right away!"

"Very well," the madam said, handing him a key. "Room Number Four."

Muggsy bolted up the stairs and nearly beat the door down. Inside the dank, foul-smelling room lay a nude hooker with her legs fully spread. Muggsy dove right in.

A few seconds later, he had to pause in his vigorous cuntlapping because he noticed that something was caught in his teeth. "How strange," he thought, after pulling the object out for examination. "A piece of corn."

Undaunted, Muggsy resumed his munching. Shortly thereafter, he was deterred again by yet another wiggling nuisance.

Clearing his gums with his finger and looking at the offending substance, he wondered, "Now when was the last time I had chipped beef?"

Finally, when Muggsy's slit-licking was interrupted

by the stringy appearance of a fried egg in his mouth, he announced to the hooker, "I think I'm going to throw up!"

After which she promptly informed him, "That's what the last guy said."

284

Q: What's the difference between a slut and a bitch?
A: A slut'll fuck anybody. A bitch will fuck anybody but you.

285

Izzy asked the Rabbi if he could borrow $40.

"Thirty dollars!" the old man cried. "What do you need $20 for?"

286

Marty was known as the welcome wagon around the prison. Whenever a new inmate was admitted, Marty would greet him and talk to him about the social activities he could look forward to on the inside. When a convict named Jake arrived, Marty asked him, "Do you like tennis?"

"Sure, I love tennis," Jake said.

"Well, then you're gonna love Mondays. . . . On Mondays they hand out rackets, and all we do the whole day is play tennis. Yeah, you'll love Mondays." Then Marty asked, "Do you like golf?"

Jake replied, "Sure, I love golf."

"Well, then you're gonna love Tuesdays. . . . On Tuesdays, we all get clubs and have a great golf tournament. Yeah, you're gonna love Tuesdays." Next Marty asked, "Do you like sex?"

"Yeah, I *love* sex!" Jake exclaimed.

"There's just one thing," Marty said. "Are you heterosexual or homosexual?"

Quickly Jake answered, "Why, I'm heterosexual, of course!"

"Well, then," Marty said, shaking his head, "you're gonna hate Wednesdays."

287

Tracy was complaining about her date to her girlfriend Emily.

"That creep called me a slut."

"That's awful!" her pal exclaimed. "What did you do?"

"I told him to get out of my bed," Tracy answered, "and take his ten friends with him!"

288

The HUSTLER Dictionary defines *specimen* as: an Italian astronaut.

289

A newlywed couple chose a romantic, candlelit restaurant for their very first dinner as husband and wife. As the waiter left their table, the wife inadvertently cracked a loud, smelly fart. To hide her embarrassment, she shouted at the waiter, "Stop that immediately!"

The waiter turned and said, "Of course, madame. In which direction was it headed?"

290

After a lifetime of celibacy, the Pope could stand no more. Sneaking into a secluded corner of the Vatican gardens, the pontiff raised his cassock, begged forgiveness, and manually relieved himself of decades' worth of sexual frustration.

Then he was interrupted by the familiar-sounding click of photographs being taken.

The Pope froze in horror as he faced a Japanese tourist snapping one picture after another of his unholy act.

"My child," the Catholic leader pleaded, "I will give

you this pinkie ring worth $5,000 in exchange for that camera!"

They made an even trade.

What a relief, the Pope thought as he returned to his chambers. On the way, he ran into one of his chief cardinals.

"Nice camera," the priest commented.

"It ought to be," the Pope declared. "I just paid $5,000 for it."

"Boy," his associate exclaimed, "whoever sold you that thing must have seen you coming!"

291

The HUSTLER Dictionary defines *lesbian opera singer* as: muff diva.

292

"It was the damnedest thing," Joe told the bartender. "The wife and I tossed a couple of coins into that wishing well at the end of the road, and then half a second later, an eighteen-wheeler jackknifed and squashed her like a bug."

"That's awful," the barkeep offered in consolation.

"You're telling me," Joe responded. "If I'd known that damn thing worked, I would have taken out a huge insurance policy on her first."

293

Q: How many Mexicans does it take to grease a car?
A: One, if you hit him right.

294

Doctor Cosgrove, a renowned gynecologist, took one look at his voluptuous new patient and abandoned his professional ethics entirely.

As he stroked the supple skin of her naked body, he asked, "Do you understand what I'm doing?"

"Yes," the patient answered. "You're checking for dermatological abrasions."

"Correct," Cosgrove lied. Next he fondled her breasts long and lovingly. Again, he inquired: "Do you understand what I'm doing?"

"You're feeling for cancerous lumps," she ventured.

"Very astute," the doctor complimented. He placed the woman's feet in stirrups, dropped his pants and slipped his dick inside her. "And do you understand what I'm doing now?"

"All too well," the patient shot back. "You're contracting herpes."

295

Q: Why did the Jews wander the desert for forty years?
A: Somebody dropped a quarter.

296

Spike stopped a man walking a three-legged pig on a leash. "Where'd you get such a weird pet?" he asked.

"This pig," the man replied, "is the most amazing animal that ever lived. One night my house caught fire, and he carried my wife and kids to safety, and put the flames out before the fire department got there."

"Wow!" Spike reacted. "But what happened to his—"

"Another time," the guy interrupted, "I was being burglarized, and this pig caught the thief in the act, returned the valuables and summoned the cops before I even got to the bottom of the stairs."

"Incredible," Spike said. "But how come—"

"Then last winter," the fellow burst in, "I fell through some ice, and this pig dragged me out and successfully revived me with CPR."

"Great!" Spike interjected, "but I have to know one thing: How come this pig's only got three legs?"

"A pig like this," the proud owner explained, "you don't eat all at once!"

297

Q: What do you call a black Frenchman?
A: Jacques Custodian.

298

A teacher known for her fanatical Christianity asked her students to name the greatest man who ever walked the face of the Earth. The one with the correct answer would win $10.

"Christopher Columbus," answered a little Italian boy.

"Saint Patrick," replied an Irish kid.

"I'm sorry, but you're both wrong," said the teacher.

Finally a Jewish boy said, "Jesus Christ."

Shocked that the youth had given the correct answer, the teacher asked the boy to come up to her desk so that he could explain his response.

"Why did you pick Jesus Christ, when you obviously don't believe in Him?" she inquired.

"Actually, I think Moses was the greatest man who ever walked the face of the Earth," the Jewish boy replied smugly. "But after all, business *is* business."

299

Q: How many male chauvinists does it take to install a kitchen lightbulb?

A: None! Let the bitch cook in the dark.

300

A strange-looking fellow walked into the local brothel, had a quick conference with the madam, and, after paying the price required for his request, was shown to a room. Inside he found an attractive prostitute naked and waiting on the bed. The man stripped, jumped up onto the bed, squatted over the woman and promptly shit on her chest. This activity continued for ten days, always with the same girl.

On the eleventh day he entered the room once more, stripped, walked over to the bed and squatted above the whore's tits. He strained and strained, but only farted.

The girl opened her eyes, looked up at him and said, "Whatsa matter, honey, don't you love me anymore?"

301

The HUSTLER Dictionary defines *extrovert* as: one pervert too many.

302

Three guys, a Frenchman, a German and a Polack, were sitting in a bar. In walked a mean-looking black guy, looking for a fight. He sat down, ordered a beer, took a drink, went over to the Frenchman and slapped him in the face, saying, "I like fucking white women."

The Frenchman looked at him and replied, "Well, that's great."

Then the big black guy went over to the German, hit him on the shoulder and said, "I like fucking white women."

The German looked at him and said, "Good for you."

The black guy sat down and took another drink of his beer. He got up, walked over to the Polack and belted him on the back, then said, "I like fucking white women." The Polack thought for a second and finally said, "I don't blame you. I don't like fucking those black ones either."

303

Q: Why do Mexicans like small steering wheels?
A: So they can drive with handcuffs on.

304

Two shepherds found themselves a particularly attractive ewe one afternoon. One of them had just climbed on and started humping when the sheep stuck her tongue out.

"Damn!" the other shepherd exclaimed. "Your prick is coming out the other end."

"Then, quick, stick another sheep on!"

305

Judge Himmelfarb stumbled home intoxicated one evening, completely oblivious to the fact that he'd thrown up on himself.

When pressed by his wife the next morning as to what happened, Himmelfarb convinced her that a belligerent drunk on the commuter train was responsible.

Later that day, the judge figured to cement his alibi by calling home with another bogus story. "You remember that drunk I told you about last night?" he asked his wife. "Well, he turned up in court, and I sentenced him to thirty days for vomiting on my jacket."

"Maybe you should give him sixty," Mrs. Himmelfarb shot back. "He shit in your pants too."

306

Q: What should you do if your girlfriend is no good at fellatio?

A: Keep pounding it into her head.

307

Sister Mary and Sister Ignatius were pounced upon by a pair of rapists on their way back to the convent.

"Forgive them, Father," Sister Mary wailed during the attack, "for they know not what they do."

"Mine does," cooed Sister Ignatius.

308

Q: How many lesbians does it take to change a light-bulb?

A: Two. One to change the bulb and one to write a folk song about it.

309

"I'm really worried about Gretchen," Harry confided to his friend Jim over the phone. "She wasn't home for dinner, and now it's almost midnight. Do you think she's okay? You know how depressed she's been since her double mastectomy."

"Relax," Jim offered. "Maybe she just went out for a drink, or dropped by a friend's house to visit."

"I don't think so," Harry intoned glumly, as he glanced at the nightstand. "She left her tits on the table."

310

A couple in their late nineties consulted an attorney about filing for divorce.

"At your age, and after nearly seventy years of marriage," the lawyer wondered, "what brought this about?"

"We wanted to wait until the children were dead," the husband answered.

311

Q: What happens when a Jew with an erection walks into a wall?

A: He breaks his nose.

312

Tomas and Serge, two gay lovers, were rear-ended by a semi as they cruised the highway.

Pulling over, Tomas instructed Serge to confront the trucker. "Tell him we're going to sue, sue, sue!" he shrieked.

Serge approached the cab and relayed the message. "Ah, why don't you just suck my cock!" the driver blurted out.

Brimming with excitement, Serge scampered back to Tomas shouting, "He wants to settle out of court!"

313

Q: What do you get when you cross a black and a WASP?

A: An abortion.

314

Two hookers were talking business.

"Have you ever been picked up by the fuzz?" asked one.

"No," said the other, "but I've been dragged around by the boobs."

315

Bill pulled up a stool at his favorite bar and announced: "My wife, Susie, must love me more than any woman has ever loved any man."

"What makes you say that?" the bartender inquired.

"Last week," Bill explained, "I had to take a couple of sick days from work, and Susie was so thrilled to have me around that every time the milkman, the cable guy and the UPS truck came by, she'd run down the driveway, waving her arms and hollering, 'My old man's home! My old man's home!' "

316

The HUSTLER Dictionary defines *vibrator* as: a slot machine.

317

Tony the nightclub owner was dazzled by the original songwriting skills of Marvin, his new piano player.

"What do you call that one, Marv?" Tony asked after an up-tempo number.

Marvin replied: "That's titled, 'Drop Your Drawers

and Sit on My Face.' Before that I played, 'Suck My Cock, and I'll Shave Your Pussy.' "

"Keep up the good work," Tony sighed, "but do me a favor, Marv: Don't announce your songs by name."

Later that evening, Marvin delighted the clubgoers for hours. Then he took a quick bathroom break, and returned to the floor.

"Excuse me, sir," a female patron called. "do you know your fly is open and your dick is hanging out?"

"Know it?" Marvin beamed. "Lady, I wrote it!"

318

Q: What do kissing and real estate have in common?
A: Location, location, location.

319

A tall, luscious blonde entered a shoe store and announced: "Bring me a pair of low heels, any style."

"What are you going to wear them with?" a clerk inquired.

"A short, fat, elderly dress manufacturer," the chippie answered.

320

The HUSTLER Dictionary defines *navel destroyer* as: a hula hoop with a nail in it.

321

In an expensive Italian restaurant, a food critic found a greasy black hair in his otherwise superb meal.

Outraged, he stormed the kitchen only to discover the chef stirring his erect penis in a pot of tomato sauce.

"Don't you have a wooden spoon?" the horrified critic winced.

"Wooden spoons we a-got," the cook blushed. "Ricotta cheese, we run out of!"

322

Little Johnny queried: "Dad, what's the difference between theory and reality?"

"Son," Johnny's father instructed, "go ask your mom if she'd fuck a stranger for a million dollars."

Johnny did as he was told, then reported: "Mom says she'd do it, Pop."

"Okay," the father chuckled. "Now pose the same question to your sister."

Little Johnny got the same response from his sister.

"It's simple," Johnny's father concluded: "In *theory*,

John, you and I share a house with a pair of million-aires, but in *reality*, we live with a couple of sluts."

323

The HUSTLER Dictionary defines *paternity suit* as: the penalty for leaving the scene of an accident.

324

Sol Rosenberg rushed his three-year-old to the emergency room.

"He swallowed several coins from my antique coin collection," Sol panicked. "Please help us!"

After more than an hour, the nurse saw that Sol had not calmed down.

"Relax, Mr. Rosenberg," she smiled. "The doctor that's handling your son is extremely skilled."

"Yes," Sol fretted, "but is he honest?"

325

Q: What's the best way to keep a hard-on?
A: Don't fuck with it.

326

A Catholic woman tearfully sought the counsel of her local priest.

"I threw my husband, Sean, out," the woman wept, "because he cheated on me. Now he swears he'll be true, and he's begging to come home. What should I do, Father?"

The reverend patted the bereaved parishioner's hand.

"The church forbids divorce," he stated, "so you'll have to forgive Sean, and give him another chance.

"But," the priest added, as his grip tightened, "you *could* get back at that bastard first . . ."

327

Q: Why are cowboy hats curved on the side?

A: So that three can fit across the front seat of a pickup truck.

328

After a night of heavy drinking, Bosco asked the bartender for directions to the men's room.

"It's a little tricky," the bartender explained, "but you go out the back door, go past the cigarette machine, and take the last door on your right. And whatever you do, don't go through the last door on your left."

Bosco stumbled out of the bar and promptly went through the wrong door. Instead of entering the men's room, he plunged down an elevator shaft that had been closed due to a flood in the building's basement.

Hearing Bosco's slurred shouts and splashes from the bottom of the flooded elevator shaft, another patron hurried over and shouted, "Hey, buddy, are you all right down there?"

"I'm okay," Bosco shouted back, "but whatever you do, don't flush!"

329

Jimbo walked into a used-car lot and asked, "is it true that my best friend, Dave, still hasn't made a single payment on that Corvette he bought from you two years ago?"

"Yeah," replied the salesman. "Are you here to make good on his account?"

"No," Jimbo answered, "I wanted to buy one for myself on those same terms."

330

When he reached the North Pole, an explorer was amazed to discover a hut with a sign on the door that read FOR MEMBERS ONLY.

When he knocked, a bearded man opened the door and barked, "This is a private club. You can only join if you do two things: Kill a polar bear and fuck an Eskimo woman."

Despite his exhaustion, the explorer set off on a new mission to gain membership to the club. Three hours later, he returned, scratched and bloodied. After catching his breath, the explorer gasped, "Okay, now where is that Eskimo woman I'm supposed to kill?"

331

The HUSTLER Dictionary defines *practical nurse* as: someone who takes care of rich, terminally ill patients by marrying them.

332

Dr. Howard, a veterinarian, came home from work one day and noticed his neighbor's eight-year-old son, Sammy, crying in the front yard.

"What's wrong, Sammy?" Dr. Howard asked.

"My folks are getting divorced," the little boy said. "My mommy told my daddy she was fed up with being married to an impotent old geezer."

Dr. Howard smiled. "You know, Sammy, sometimes horses get the same problem your dad has. I've got some pills for curing horses that should help your dad too. You take one pill, break it in half, and mix it up with your dad's food. He'll be cured in no time."

Two months later, Dr. Howard saw Sammy crying

again in his front yard. "What's wrong now, Sammy?" Dr. Howard asked.

"Don't even ask," the little boy mumbled. "Mommy's dead, my sister's pregnant, my ass is burning, and our dog is too scared to come home."

333

Q: Why was the homo fired from his position at the sperm bank?

A: He was drinking on the job.

334

One day a man went into a restaurant and ordered a bowl of soup. The waitress brought his order out to him on a tray, with her middle finger immersed in the middle of his soup bowl.

"What the hell's the idea of putting your finger in my bowl of soup?" the man bellowed at the waitress.

"My doctor said the best thing for my rheumatism was to keep my finger pressed in a warm, damp place," the waitress informed him.

"Oh, yeah," the man shouted, "then why don't you take that finger of yours and shove it up your fat ass?"

"I'm sorry, sir," the waitress replied, "but I already tried that before I brought your soup out."

335

Q: Why do black women have to lug around such big
  purses?

A: They need them to carry their lipstick.

336

Hungrier'n shit, a guy plopped down at the lunch
counter next to a young man who had a steaming bowl
of chili in front of him. When the waitress came to take
his order, the man said, "That chili smells pretty good.
Lemme have a bowl of that." The waitress brought his
order right away, and the man scarfed it down as fast as
he could shovel it in. Still hungry, he noticed that the
young man beside him hadn't touched his bowl. "Hey,
man," he asked, "you gonna eat that?"

"Nope."

"Ya mind if I have at it, then?"

The young man shrugged and said, "Fuck, go
ahead." The man thanked him, slid the bowl over and
dug in. He was almost through when he looked down
and noticed a greasy dog turd lying in the bottom of the
bowl. Gagging, he power-puked his meal back up into
the bowl. The young man next to him glanced over and
said, "Yeah, that's as far as I got, too."

337

The HUSTLER Dictionary defines *K-Y jelly* as: logjam.

338

Three bank robbers were talking in their hideout. "You know," one said, "I can put eight beer cans on my cock when it's hard."

"Big deal," the second said. "I can lay ten silver dollars along mine when it's hard."

"Twelve crows can perch on mine when it's hard," boasted the third.

Just then, the police opened fire. A barrage of bullets whizzed overhead and tear gas rounds exploded all around. "I gotta tell the truth," the first terrified crook shouted above the din. "I can only put three beer cans on my cock when it's hard."

"To be honest," the second admitted, "I can only lay three silver dollars along mine when it's hard."

"Okay, okay," the third screamed after another thunderous volley, "the twelfth crow has to stand on one foot!"

339

Q: Why is a clitoris like Antarctica?
A: Most men know it's there, but few men really care.

340

A man arrived home early to find his wife in the arms of his best friend. To calm the shocked husband, the friend suggested they play gin rummy. "If I win," he said, "you have to get a divorce so I can marry her. If you win, I promise never to see her again."

"Okay," agreed the husband, "but how about a penny a point to make it interesting?"

341

An old man checked into a retirement hotel that had six women for every man staying there. He was approached by a woman in her mid-seventies. "So, are you married?" asked the old woman.

"I was married once," the man replied. "I killed my wife with an ax and spread her body parts all over town. I got caught and went to jail for a long time. In jail I killed another convict and shot a guard while trying to escape. I finally got out after fifty-five years. In fact, I was just released yesterday."

"Oh, so you're single," she cooed.

342

A pilot and a blind man went up in an airplane. The pilot had a heart attack and died. The blind man radioed, "Mayday, Mayday!" to the tower. "We have a dead pilot, I'm blind, and we're flying upside down!" he screamed.

"How do you know you're upside down if you're blind?" the tower asked.

"Because the shit's running down my collar!"

343

Q: What do you get when you cross a woman who has PMS with a woman who has ESP?

A: A bitch who thinks she knows everything.

344

Every night the man would stagger home drunk, and his wife would meet him at the door to give him a real tongue-lashing. One day, some of her friends told her that she was going about it all wrong.

"When he comes home next time," they told her, "have a sandwich ready for him, and treat him nicely."

She figured it was worth a shot. When he came home that night, she greeted him pleasantly. "I'm so happy to see you, baby. Why don't we go into the kitchen have a bite to eat, talk for a bit and then go to bed?"

"Okay, why not?" he slurred. "I'm gonna catch hell when I get home anyway."

345

Q: What are the three major political parties in the United States?

A: Democratic, Republican and Cocktail.

346

The old graybeard walked up to the hot, little jailbait number at the bar and said, "Where have you been all my life, sweet thing?"

"Teething," she replied.

347

The HUSTLER Dictionary defines *Florida* as: God's waiting room.

348

Jonathan Gold was driving down the street with his family when they saw a sign on an evangelical Christian church that said, "Give your life to Jesus— $500 reward to converts."

The deal was too good to pass up; so Gold pulled over to the church, rushed inside, converted to Christianity and collected his reward. When he got back into the car, his wife said, "That's a lot of money. I want a fur coat."

His daughter chimed in, "I want diamond earrings."

His son said, "I need a new bike."

Gold shook his head sadly. "It's always the same story. We Gentiles get some money and you Jews want to take it away."

349

An avid golfer hit his ball into the woods. When he went to look for it, he stumbled upon a leprechaun brewing up a mysterious concoction.

"What are you making?" asked the golfer.

"This is a magic brew," said the leprechaun, "and if you drink it, your golf game will improve remarkably. You'll never lose again."

"That's great—let me have some!" cried the golfer.

"Have as much as you like, but I must warn you, there is one serious side effect: It will almost certainly diminish your sexual desires."

"I can live with that," responded the golfer, and he gulped the potion down.

To his utter delight, the golfer found that it actually worked. He won every match, and in six months found himself the club champion. He was so happy that he decided to look for the leprechaun in order to thank him.

"It worked!" said the golfer. "It really did! I'm now the club champion!"

"Yes, but what about your sex life?" questioned the leprechaun.

"It's okay," answered the golfer. "I've had sex three or four times in the past six months."

"That doesn't sound very good to me."

"Hey, it's not bad at all, for a Catholic priest in a small parish."

350

Q: Where are two places that even the most undesirable people can get laid?

A: Prison and animal shelters.

351

A young hillbilly went to a whorehouse for his first lay. When he told the madam he was a virgin, she showed him how to put on a rubber, rolling it down on her thumb. The young man trotted upstairs. After he fucked the girl, she said, "That rubber must have broken. I feel all wet inside."

The rube held up his thumb and said, "No, it didn't. It's just as good as new."

352

The rugrat walked into the living room and asked, "Pop, can I have $10 to buy a guinea pig?"

The biker told his son, "Kid, here's 20 bucks. Go find a nice Irish girl."

353

Joe found himself in bed with a sensationally hot chick. The trouble was that her big, tough-looking husband lay snoring away right next to them.

"Are you sure he won't wake up?" Joe inquired of his horny conquest as she spread her legs.

"He sleeps like a rock," the woman answered. "Pull a hair out of his ass, and you'll see: He won't budge."

Joe reached over and plucked a hair from the slumbering man's butt. Nothing happened. Satisfied that they'd be uninterrupted, Joe plowed into his pickup.

When he was ready for a second go, Joe asked again, "Are you sure your husband won't notice us?"

"Yank another hair out," the babe sighed, "then maybe you'll believe me."

Joe followed her instruction once again. They repeated this ritual throughout the evening: Joe would remove a hair from the dude's butt crack, and then he'd screw the wife.

Finally, as Joe reached for hair number seven, the husband sprang to life, roaring: "Listen, pal—I don't care how many times you bang my old lady, but do you have to keep count on my ass?"

354

Q: Why did the Mexicans fight so hard to capture the Alamo?

A: So they would have four clean walls to write on.

355

Officer Sullivan demanded to know what was going on with the wino whose fingers were wedged deep up another bum's ass.

"My buddy's sick," the wino explained. "I'm trying to make him throw up."

"You ought to put your finger down his throat," Sullivan advised. "Tickling his sphincter won't make him puke."

"*Au contraire*, officer," the wino replied. "Right after I get my hand good and coated, *then* I'll stick it down his throat!"

356

The HUSTLER Dictionary defines *CUNT* as: Cannot Understand Normal Thinking.

357

After catching Clem with Mrs. Brown in the hay, Farmer Brown grabbed his shotgun and hollered: "Clem, I'm gonna blow your balls off!"

"Please, old friend," the terrified Clem begged, "just give me a chance!"

"All right," Farmer Brown chuckled. "Swing 'em!"

358

A statuesque blonde walked into a dinner party on the arm of a bald, elderly, scowling tycoon.

A society lady approached the young lovely to admire the huge shimmering gemstone hanging around her neck.

"I must tell you," the matron exclaimed, "that you are wearing the most incredible piece of jewelry I have ever seen."

"That," the blonde responded, "is the one-and-only Blanton diamond."

"I'm surprised I've never heard of it," the woman marveled. "I study famous gems as a hobby."

"Well," the chippy revealed, "the Blanton diamond has an ancient, unspeakably evil curse attached to it."

"Really?" the woman queried. "What could that be?"

The blonde grimaced and gestured toward the tycoon. "Mr. Blanton, over there."

359

Q: What is the difference between a brownnose and a shithead?

A: Depth perception.

360

"I've been married three times, and I'm still a virgin," Debbie complained to her new friend. "My first husband was a college professor—he only talked about it. My second husband was a doctor, and all he ever wanted to do was look at it."

"And what about your third husband?" asked her amazed friend.

"He was a gourmet," came the reply.

361

The HUSTLER Dictionary defines *catcher's mask* as: French chastity belt.

362

Mrs. Frank came home and found her husband in bed with a lady midget. She started to cry, whimpering, "Two weeks ago you promised me you wouldn't do this anymore."

Mr. Frank looked up sheepishly and said, "Well, dear, you must admit—I *am* tapering off."

363

A biker went to Las Vegas for the annual Jerry Lewis Telethon, arriving at the studio with two enormous suitcases. "I'm carrying $1 million in cash for Jerry's kids," he declared.

"A million dollars?" asked the astonished producer. "That's a lot of money—let's have a look."

Proudly, the biker opened one of the suitcases, which contained twenty thousand $50 bills.

"I've never seen that much cash!" the producer exclaimed. "How'd you raise it?"

"It wasn't easy," replied the biker. "For the past six months, I've been visiting men's restrooms all across the country. I stand beside them at the urinal and say, 'Ya better give me a hundred bucks for Jerry's kids, or I'll cut your balls off with my Buck knife.' I did this for eight hours a day, and that's how I raised the money."

"That's unbelievable," said the producer. "A million dollars in cash! And what's in the other suitcase?"

"Well," said the biker, "some didn't give . . ."

364

Q: What would be the best thing about electing a woman President?

A: We wouldn't have to pay her as much.

365

A woman was discussing her divorce with her lawyer. "Don't you love him anymore?" the attorney asked.

"Oh, I still love him," she replied, "but all he ever wants is sex. I can't take it."

"Instead of divorcing him, why don't you try charging him every time he wants to make love?" the lawyer suggested.

The exhausted wife decided to give the plan a try. As soon as she walked into the house that night, her husband said, "Okay, let's go."

"Not so fast," she said. "I'm going to charge you from now on. Five dollars in the kitchen, ten dollars in the living room, and twenty-five in the bedroom."

"Well, then, here's twenty-five bucks," he said, slapping the cash into her hand. The wife began walking to the bedroom.

"Hold on," he said, grabbing her hand. "That'll be five times in the kitchen!"

366

Allan was sitting at a bar in a Miami Beach hotel feeling exceedingly horny, when a beautiful hooker approached him.

"How much do you want?" asked Allan.

"One hundred dollars for the entire evening," replied the hooker.

"Well, if I'm going to pay that kind of money, you must do it under my rules."

She said, "Honey, that's fine, as long as you're paying."

Allan said, "Okay, meet me in my room in ten minutes, and we'll close the drapes, turn out the lights and do it in pitch-black darkness."

"That's okay, honey. It's your money."

When they got together in the room, Allan really gave it to her. Then he said, "Let's rest a few moments," and then he started in again. The same scene went on for two hours. Finally, after six encounters, Allan seemed even stronger than before.

The hooker said, "Allan, you are the most fantastic lover I have ever had. You just keep getting better and better every time."

"Listen lady," said a voice. "My name is Daniel. Allan is outside selling your ass at 50 bucks a throw."

367

Q: What is the difference between an Iraqi woman and a catfish?

A: One has whiskers and smells bad, and the other lives in water.

368

"I think my wife is pissed at me," said the man to his co-worker. "I made a slip of the tongue this morning."

"Oh," the co-worker asked, "how's that?"

"I was sitting across the table from my wife at breakfast and meant to say, 'Honey, would you pass the milk?' but what came out instead was, 'You scroungy bitch, you've really fucked my life!' "

369

Q: What's the difference between fucking a girl with arms and fucking a girl without arms?

A: If you're fucking a girl without arms and your dick slips out, you have to put it back in yourself.

370

A man returned home from the graveyard shift a 7 a.m., went straight to the bedroom and found his wife with the sheet pulled over her head, feigning sleep. Not to be denied, the horny man pulled up the sheet and proceeded to screw her.

Afterward, he hurried to the kitchen for something to eat and was startled to find breakfast on the table and his wife pouring coffee. "How'd you get in here so fast?" he asked. "We were just screwin' in the bedroom a couple minutes ago!"

"Oh, my God!" his wife gasped. "That's my mother! She came over and spent the night in our bed." Rushing into the bedroom, she cried, "Mother, I can't believe this happened. Why didn't you say something?"

"I haven't spoken to that bum for twenty years," she huffed, "and I wasn't about to start now."

371

The HUSTLER Dictionary defines *loneliness* as: being the first homosexual.

372

The bank manager saw a new employee diligently counting out $100 bills. "You look to be on your way up to executive," he said. "Where did you receive your business education?"

"Yale," the fellow replied, still counting out bills.

"That's excellent," the manager said. "And what's your name?"

"Yim Yohnson."

373

Q: What's worth more than Jack Ruby's .38 Special pistol at auction?

A: Lyndon B. Johnson's canceled check to Lee Harvey Oswald.

374

A fellow walked into his doctor's office with his hand horribly mangled. The doctor looked at the injury and said, "I'll give you a shot of Novocain, and in just a minute I'll fix you right up."

"Don't worry about the shot, Doc," the man replied. "Just fix it—I've had pain worse than this twice before."

After the doctor had finished his work, he asked the guy what kind of pain was worse than getting a gash that went to the bone sewn up without any anesthesia.

"A few years ago," the guy began, "I was in the north woods hunting. I sat down behind a bush to take a crap, when my balls fell into a bear trap."

Stunned, the doctor cried, "Oh, my God, that must have been terrible! What could possibly have hurt worse than that?"

The guy answered, "I ran out of chain on that bear trap."

375

A guy was taking a leak in the men's room when another fellow entered with his arms held out from his sides, bent at an awkward angle, and came over to him. "Would you do me a favor and unzip my pants?" he asked.

Figuring the fellow to be crippled, the guy obliged, but not without some embarrassment. Then the fellow asked that the guy take out his pecker and hold it while he drained his kidney.

"Give it a shake," came the next request, "then zip it up for me." The guy obliged.

"Say, thanks," said the queer, flouncing to the door, "I guess my nails are dry now."

376

Fred went to his longtime physician, complaining of memory problems. "I just hope it's not Alzheimer's," confessed Fred. "See, I'm getting terribly forgetful. I lose track of where I'm going or what I'm supposed to do when I get there. What do you think I should do?"

"Well, the first thing you need to do," replied his doctor, "is pay me in advance . . ."

377

Q: If it only takes one sperm to fertilize an egg, why does a man come so much?

A: So he can leave a bad taste in a woman's mouth.

378

The old man woke up one night, and to his utter amazement found his pecker hard as a rock for the first time in many years. He shook his wife's shoulder until she woke up, then showed her his enormous boner.

"You see that thing, woman?" he said proudly. "What do you think we ought to do with it?"

With one eye open, his wife replied, "Well, now that you got all the wrinkles out of it, this might be a good time to wash it."

379

A Frenchman and a Polack were in the woods hunting when suddenly a voluptuous, blond girl raced across their path, totally nude.

"Boy, would I love to eat that!" the Frenchman exclaimed.

So the Polack shot her.

380

One night the Pope was saying his bedtime prayers when God Himself came down from heaven to listen to them. Afterward, God sat down on the Pope's bed and said, "Listen, you've been such a good Pope and devoted follower that I'm going to eliminate anything in the world that displeases you."

The Pope was overcome with emotion. For a brief moment he couldn't think of anything to say, but then he confessed to one thing that was really getting to him.

"As you know, God," he said, "I'm very attached to my country of origin. The one thing that really irritates me is all those Polish jokes."

"No problem," God replied. "From this moment on, there shall be no more Polish jokes. Is there anything else you'd like me to do away with before I return to heaven?"

The Pope thought and thought and finally said, "Chocolate-covered peanuts!"

"Well, I always thought they were harmless," replied God, "but if it really means that much to you, I'll get rid of them."

"Well, you see," said the Pope, "I'm not getting any younger, and it's getting harder and harder to peel 'em."

381

Q: What's the smelliest thing in the world?
A: An anchovy's pussy.

382

Three winos huddled under a bridge and broke open a couple of jugs. After drinking for several hours, they passed out. In the morning, two woke up to find that the third had died during the night.

At the funeral home, the two surviving friends stood

by the coffin of their departed buddy. "Boy, ol' George sure looks bad, don't he?" the first remarked.

"Well, damn, he should," the second replied. "He ain't had a fuckin' drink in three days!"

383

"Mr. Spencer," the banker said to the oil man, "we lent you $1 million to revive your old wells, and they went dry."

"Coulda been worse," the oil man replied.

"Then we lent you a million more to drill new wells," the banker continued, "and they were dry."

"Coulda been worse."

"And then we lent you another million for new drilling equipment, and it all broke down."

"Coulda been worse."

"I'm getting a little tired of hearing that, Mr. Spencer," the banker snapped. "Tell me, just how could it have been worse?"

"Coulda been *my* money."

384

Four businessmen traveled to Las Vegas for a convention, but on the first night of carousing, the meek one of the group decided to stay in. While sitting on his bed at the hotel, he reached over, grabbed an ornamental lamp and rubbed it for a laugh. To his surprise, a genie flowed out and asked him what his wish was. The mild-mannered, slight fellow explained his request, and the genie said, before returning to the lamp, "As you wish." A moment later the man heard a knock at the door, and there stood three hooded Klansmen. The one holding a noose stepped forward and asked, "You the one who wanted to be hung like a Negro?"

385

The HUSTLER Dictionary defines *feminine-hygiene spray* as: around-the-cock protection.

386

A little man rushed into the police station one night and announced, "I pushed my wife down a flight of stairs. Throw me in jail."

The desk sergeant asked, "Did you kill her?"

"I'm pretty sure I didn't," the suspect replied. "That's why I need you to lock me up."

387

During his first three-month evaluation, a rookie cop mentioned to the chief of police that the stress of the job was really starting to wear him down. The chief told the young policeman that whenever he was feeling too tense, he's go home and screw the living hell out of his wife for about an hour, which always made him feel better and enabled him to return to work with a much better outlook. The rookie considered this piece of wisdom and said it sounded like good advice; he'd give it a try and see if it helped.

The next week the chief called the kid in and asked how things were going. The new cop replied that, in fact, just that morning he'd experienced extreme stress and had followed his boss's suggestion, with great success. He felt great. After being dismissed by his pleased superior, the rookie abruptly halted at the door and said, "Oh, Chief, I almost forgot. Your wife asked me to tell you to pick up some lamb chops for dinner."

388

A cowboy parked his truck at the curb and walked into a bar for a cold brew to wash the dust down. Looking around, he noticed that all the stools had numbers painted on their backs. After ordering a tall one, he asked the guy sitting next to him, "What's the deal with the numbered seats, man?"

"Well," the guy said, "every hour they call out a number, and if it's yours, you get to go in the back and get laid."

"Aw, bullshit," the cowboy snorted. "Tell me, has your number ever been called?"

"No," the guy replied, "but I know it's on the level, 'cause they've called my wife's number four times already."

389

Q: What's the hardest part of a male-to-female sex-change operation?

A: Sewing in the anchovy.

390

"Why are you so down?" Wade asked a depressed man at the health club. "When I saw you here yesterday, you were arm in arm with that gorgeous aerobics instructor."

"Well, we went to her place and had a few drinks," the man explained. "Then she said, 'Marvin, take off my blouse,' and a moment later, 'Marvin, take off my leotard!' Before long, she said, 'Marvin, take off my bra!' Then, finally, she said 'Oh, Marvin, take off my panties!'"

"Oh, you had it made!" Wade moaned enviously. "Was it great?"

"I suppose so. But after that, I couldn't see past Marvin!"

391

One night two friends, Bob and John, were in the local bar absolutely shitfaced when Bob decided to call it quits and go home. Taking a shortcut through the local graveyard, Bob fell into a freshly dug grave.

An hour later John left for home and took the same shortcut. While staggering through the graveyard, he heard a faint voice calling, "Help! Help! Somebody please help me!"

John stumbled over to the open grave, looked down and said, "Hey, Bob! What's going on?"

Looking up, Bob spotted John and cried out, "Thank God! Help me out. It's cold down here."

John looked around at the mound of freshly dug earth, then at his friend and said, "No damn wonder you're cold. You've kicked off your dirt!"

392

The HUSTLER Dictionary defines *oral sex* as: genital slurpees.

393

To show his undying love for his girlfriend, Wendy, Jim had her name tattooed on his cock. The tattoo was arranged so that when his cock was fully erect, the whole name was visible, but when it was limp, only the letters W and Y could be seen.

A few months later, while vacationing in Jamaica, Jim was taking a piss in the bathroom of a bar. Next to him was a Rastafarian, also taking a leak. Glancing down, Jim saw, to his amazement, the letters W and Y tattooed on the Rasta's cock.

"Hey," he said, "do you have a girlfriend named Wendy too?"

"No, mon," the Rasta replied. "Mine says, 'Welcome to Jamaica. Have a Nice Day!' "

394

As a highway patrolman approached an accident site, he found that the entire driver's side of a BMW had been ripped away, taking with it the driver's arm.

The injured yuppie, obviously in shock, kept moaning, "My car, my car," as the officer tried to comfort him.

"Sir," the patrolman said gently, "I think we should be more concerned about your arm than your car."

The driver looked down to where his arm should have been, then screamed, "My Rolex! My Rolex!"

395

A bereaved husband was standing in the funeral home next to his wife's casket, greeting friends and relatives.

Finally, his older brother came up and told him they had to talk in private. When they got out into the hall, the brother said, "Everybody's gossiping like crazy. Why in the hell did you choose a Y-shaped casket for Margaret?"

"Well," the man said, "I came home and found her nude in bed. For once she wasn't bitching that she had a headache, so I took off my clothes and climbed on. It wasn't until *rigor mortis* set in that I noticed she was dead, and by then it was too late to get her legs together."

396

Q: What's a Puerto Rican limousine?

A: A garbage truck with Mercedes hubcaps.

397

On the eve of his transfer to Rome, an Irish priest paid a visit to the Kellys, who had been childless for six years, promising to light a candle for them at the Vatican.

Thirteen years later he returned to Ireland, dropped in on the Kellys and found nine children romping around the house. Congratulating Mrs. Kelly on her fruitfulness, the priest looked around and asked, "But where is Mr. Kelly?"

"Sean?" the haggard woman said, "Oh, he went to Rome to blow out the candle."

398

Two gays were standing on the San Francisco Bay Bridge, watching the ships go by. They were in disagreement as to the type of ship passing at the time. A policeman happened to be walking by, so they called him over and asked what kind of ship it was. He looked over the rail at it and told them it was a ferryboat.

One gay looked at the other in surprise and said, "Gee, I didn't know we had a navy."

399

Q: What does a man have that is white and twelve inches long?

A: Nothing.

400

A man with an extreme case of hiccups walked into a bank and asked an attractive cashier to cash a personal check for $10.

"I'm sorry, sir," apologized the young lady. "but my records show that your checking account is overdrawn by $200."

"You've got to be kidding!" exclaimed the man.

"Yes," agreed the cashier. "But I cured your hiccups."

"Damned if you didn't," replied the customer. "Now, do you happen to have a clean pair of underwear?"

401

Two hunters were off on their annual trip to the Canadian wilderness to bag moose. As the seaplane landed on a lake in a remote area, the pilot said, "I'll be back in one week to pick you up. But only one moose, please."

When he returned to the lake, he found the hunters proudly standing beside two moose. "I told you guys only one moose!" the furious flier screamed. "There's no way the plane can take off with that much weight!"

"You're just a chicken pilot," one hunter said. "We killed two moose last year, and that pilot wasn't afraid to take off."

Stung by the suggestion of cowardice, the pilot reconsidered. "All right, if you did it last year, I guess we can try it."

So they loaded up, and the pilot taxied to the far end of the lake to begin his takeoff. The plane bounced across the water as it strained to get airborne, but the overloaded aircraft finally ran out of space and crashed into the trees.

Sometime later, the hunters regained consciousness. "Where are we?" one asked.

His friend looked around at the scattered debris, then back at the edge of the lake, and replied, "Oh, I guess about a hundred yards farther than last year."

402

Q: How many Teamsters does it take to change a light-bulb?

A: Five. You gotta problem with that?!

403

A hillbilly visited his son about a week after the boy got married. "Well, son," he said, "how do you like married life?"

"Ain't married no more, Pa," the boy answered. "I killed her on our wedding night. I shot her dead."

"Why in the hell did you do that?" the old man asked.

"Well, Daddy, I found out she was a virgin, and I figured if she wasn't good enough for her own family, she wasn't good enough for ours."

404

A traveler was surprised to see spaghetti and meatballs offered at a small-town restaurant in Mexico. He ordered the dish and was especially delighted with the meatballs. Before leaving, he went to the kitchen to congratulate the chef and, if possible, get the recipe. The chef was reluctant to part with the recipe, but after much coaxing, he admitted that his brother ran the local bullring and that he used the male portions of the defeated bulls for his ingredients.

Months later the traveler revisited the town and once again ordered the spagetti and meatballs. This time the meatballs' quality was not nearly as good as the first, and the traveler complained to the chef. Embarrassed, the cook scuffed his feet and said, "Señor, you must understand, sometimes the bull wins too."

405

The HUSTLER Dictionary defines *miracle whip* as: successful masturbation by a 90-year-old man.

406

A rabbi and a priest were seated together on a cross-country flight. When an attractive flight attendant asked them if they would like cocktails, the rabbi said, "Yes, I'd like a Manhattan, please."

"No, thank you," the priest said, turning to explain to his seatmate. "As a priest, I can't drink or fornicate."

"Wait a second," the rabbi said, standing and waving at the flight attendant. "I didn't know I had a choice."

407

The HUSTLER Dictionary defines *pedophilia* as: minor offensives.

408

A doctor was examining a luscious 16-year-old girl.

"My breasts hurt," she complained to him.

He examined and fondled her small but firm boobs. "That's only natural," he told her. "They're just growing. They'll get bigger."

"Something else bothers me. I'm getting hair under my arms."

The doc looked and answered, "That's natural," then took off his shirt and showed her his bushy underarms. "You'll get more hair, like me."

"But I'm also getting hair here," whispered the girl, shyly pointing to her crotch.

"Let me see," said the doc as he washed his hands.

She dropped her panties and said, "See."

The doc looked, felt and huskily said, "That's only natural. Your hair will grow thicker, like mine." He then dropped his pants and pointed to his crotch.

The girl saw his throbbing erection and exclaimed, "And when am I gonna get one of those?"

"Just as soon as I pull down the shades."

409

The HUSTLER Dictionary defines *epileptic seizure* as: a thrash dance.

410

A couple who had five children went to see a gynecologist and asked what he could recommend to keep the wife from getting pregnant again. The doctor gave the husband some rubbers and told him to place one on his organ before having intercourse.

Two months later the couple were back in the doctor's office; the wife was expecting once again. The puzzled physician examined his patient, then asked the husband, "Didn't you put a rubber on your organ before intercourse the way I told you to?"

"Well, not exactly," the husband replied. "You see, we don't have an organ; so we just laid one on the piano."

411

Q: What is the miracle of AIDS?
A: It turns fruits into vegetables.

412

A small-town country lawyer and his wife were out taking a walk when a hip, flashily dressed young female passed by and shouted a sexy "Hiya, Sam" at him.

The lawyer, his face reddening, gave a mild "How do" and walked on.

"And who was that?" asked his suspicious wife, her lips tightening slightly into an angry scowl.

"Oh, just . . . a young woman I met—professionally," he answered sheepishly.

"Oh, yeah?" she queried. "Your profession or hers?"

413

When the boy came into the school playground, he found his friend sitting in the corner, shaking like a leaf. "What happened, Billy?" the boy asked,

"I was walking down Main Street," Billy answered, "when that big bully from the seventh grade started to chase me. I turned down the alley, but he slid around the corner after me. Then I ran down Elm and around the corner, but he slid after me again."

"Wow!" the first boy exclaimed. "If I'd been you, I would have shit in my pants!"

"What do you think that bully was sliding on?"

414

Q: What's pink and hairy and sits on a wall?

A: Humpty Cunt.

415

Macho Joe walked into a singles bar and sat down next to a very attractive girl. "How would you feel about the two of us engaging in a little oral sex?"

"It depends," the girl replied. "Your face or mine?"

416

A little Jewish guy who couldn't have weighed more than seventy pounds went to Houston on business. He checked into a hotel that was fifty-stories high and was shown into a suite the size of a ballroom.

Overwhelmed, he went down to the bar and was served a drink in a glass so large, he needed both hands to lift it. "Everything's big in Texas, pal," said the bartender with a wink.

When the fellow's steak dinner arrived, the plate was completely covered by the meat. "Hey, everything's big in Texas," said the waiter.

Completely overcome, the little guy decided it was time to hit his super-king-size bed, but he lost his way in the hotel's vast corridors. Opening the door of a darkened room, he fell into the hotel swimming pool.

"Whatever you do," he sputtered, "don't flush!"

417

The HUSTLER Dictionary defines *Polish vibrator* as: a mop handle and six relatives shaking the bed.

418

A pretty, voluptuous high school girl led an active sex life despite a mild heart condition that flared up from time to time. One evening she brought her latest flame home to dinner. Her father, oblivious to his daughter's past sexual exploits but suspecting she might be getting serious with her dinner guest, took it upon himself to say a few words to the young man. Concerned that she was perhaps hiding her heart condition from her suitor, the father approached him during a lull in the evening.

"I think there is something about my daughter you should know," her father said as the boy's face turned fearful. "She has acute angina."

"Yeah, I know," replied the boy with an impish grin. "And she's got a great pair of tits too!"

419

Driving through the Australian outback, an American tourist and his wife pulled over to watch the amazing sight of a bushman running down a kangaroo on foot. Almost out of breath, the bushman eventually caught the kangaroo and proceeded to ravish it with gusto.

The tourists drove on, shaking their heads with amazement. Over the next hill they came upon a stockman on horseback running down another kangaroo, which he promptly raped.

Soon the couple came to a little town, where they stopped at a bar to quench their thirst. The man went into the restroom to relieve himself and came upon a fellow with one leg who was leaning against the wall next to his crutches and masturbating like crazy.

The tourist hurried back into the bar and stared at the barman. "What kind of a country is this?" he asked. "Back up the road we saw a man catch and rape a kangaroo! Then a little farther along we saw another man run a kangaroo down and rape it! Just now I went into the restroom and found a man with one leg, pulling on himself like the end of the world was near! What the hell is going on?"

The barman stated back, incredulous. "Well, mate, you certainly don't expect a bloke with only one leg to run a kangaroo down, do you?"

420

An old black man was lying on his deathbed, holding a conversation with the Lord. After screwing up enough courage, he finally asked a question he had wanted to know the answer to for years.

"Lord," the old man queried, "is You black, or is You white?"

The Lord replied, "I am what I am."

"Please don't jive me," the old man said. "I needs to know. Is You black, or is You white?"

"My son," the Lord replied, "if I were black, I would have said 'I is what I is.' "

421

The HUSTLER Dictionary defines *cold cream* as: a vaginal lubricant for necrophiles.

422

A 90-year-old woman and a 93-year-old man had just gotten married. When the husband came out of the bathroom ready for bed, he found his wife standing on her head and up against the bedroom wall.

"What the hell are you doing?" he asked.

"Well," she explained, "I figured in case you couldn't get it up, you could just drop it in."

423

A homosexual went mountain climbing, slipped off the edge of a cliff and caught hold of a low-hanging branch about ten feet below the place from which he had fallen. Knowing he was going to die, he fervently began praying to the Lord to save him.

Much to the fellow's relief, an angel appeared and asked, "Do you truly believe in the Lord?"

"Oh, yes," answered the gay, "with all my heart."

"Then let go," the angel said, "and the Lord will save you."

The man thought about it for a moment, then let go and fell to his death. The angel looked down at his handiwork and exclaimed, "Shit! The way I hate fags, I'll never know how I got to be an angel."

424

Two ladies were out driving in the Virginia countryside, fifty miles from Washington, D.C. One of them noticed two naked men in a field masturbating each other, and she pointed them out to her friend.

"Look!" the woman exclaimed. "Two Democrats jerking each other off."

"How do you know they're Democrats?" her friend asked.

"If they were Republicans, they'd be fucking a crowd of poor people."

425

The HUSTLER Dictionary defines *holy oil* as: preacher cum.

426

A Ku Klux Klansman in full attire walked into a bowling alley carrying a baseball bat. With a fanatic gleam in his eye he strode up to the nearest rack of bowling balls and began energetically beating on the balls with his bat.

The manager of the bowling alley ran over to him and angrily demanded, "What the hell are you doing?"

"Don't try to stop me!" the Klansman roared. "I gotta get these niggers before they hatch!"

427

Four unfortunate Polish sailors recently lost their lives. One died at sea, and the other three drowned trying to dig his grave.

428

On his deathbed a man confessed to his wife, "Honey, I've been unfaithful to you, but every time I cheated, I put a dollar under the rug. All the money is still there except the one dollar that I spent for medicine."

Surprisingly, the man recovered, but his wife took sick. She also felt she should confess; so she told him, "I was unfaithful to you too, dear, but every time I cheated, I dropped a pea through the little hole in the kitchen floor. They are all still under the house—except the three bushels we ate during hard times last winter."

429

The HUSTLER Dictionary defines *super-lover* as: a guy with a 9-inch tongue who can breathe through his ears.

430

The Italian and Polish paratroopers were arguing about who was best at packing a parachute. Unable to resolve the dispute on the ground, they decided to go up in a plane and judge by the midair performances of their chutes. The Pole went first, pulled the cord and started floating toward the earth. Then the Italian jumped, pulled the cord and nothing happened. He pulled the safety cord again—still nothing.

In a matter of seconds the Italian whizzed past the Pole, plummeting downward like a stone. "Oh!" shouted the Pole, yanking off his harness. "So ya wanna race!"

431

The blind man walked into a department store with his seeing-eye dog and headed straight for the men's underwear department.

Surrounded by pajamas and boxer shorts, he came to a stop, picked up his German shepherd by its hind legs and began swinging the dog around in a circle.

A startled clerk ran over to him and asked loudly, "Sir, . . . may I help you with anything?"

"No, thanks," the man answered. "Just looking."

432

A: How does a Yuppie couple fuck doggy-style?

A: The man sits up and begs, and the woman rolls over and plays dead.

433

A man was sitting in the local porn-movie house when suddenly he smelled an awful stench. He noticed a drunk sitting a couple of seats away, and he realized that the odor was coming from that direction.

"Hey, asshole," the man called, "did you shit in your pants?"

"Yeah," the derelict replied.

"Well, what the fuck are you going to do about it?" the man demanded.

"Don't know yet," the drunk answered. "I haven't finished."

434

Sam phoned Ron in the middle of the night. "My piles are killing me! And I can't go to the doctor till tomorrow morning!"

"Listen," said Ron, "get a tea bag and put it on your asshole. It will shrink the swelling. Take a sleeping pill, and tomorrow you can go to the doctor."

Sam followed his friend's advice. The next day he rushed to a proctologist, who immediately had him get up on the examination table. The doctor spread Sam's cheeks and muttered, "Hmmm."

"Something wrong?" asked Sam.

"No," answered the doctor. "You're going to take a long trip . . . You're going to meet a tall, dark . . ."

435

Three little kids were sitting on a curb one day—a Catholic boy, a Jewish boy and a black boy. A priest walked up to the group, and the Catholic jumped up. The priest asked him, "What are the two most important things in your life?"

"The Virgin Mary and you, Father."

Later a rabbi came up to the group and asked the

same question. The Jewish lad answered, "King David and you, Rabbi."

A little while after that the black youngster leaned over to his friends and asked, "What's the matter, y'all never heard of watermelon and pussy?"

436

One Sunday a wino decided to get out of the city for some fresh country air. He found a beautiful field and lay back in a haystack to relax and enjoy his surroundings. In a short while he noticed a crop duster flying an erratic pattern overhead. Trying to land, the plane bounced hard, tipped over, broke a wing and hit a barn.

The wino ran over to see if he could be of any help. As he neared the barn, he saw a man come stumbling out, clothes in rags and holding his broken arm.

"Hey, buddy," the wino yelled, "are you all right?"

"I'm just fine, my good man," the guy answered. "God is my copilot."

"In that case," the wino replied, "you'd better let Him fly, 'cause you're gonna kill yourself!"

437

A Polack came home and found his wife in bed with the milkman. He rushed into the closet, pulled out a gun and pointed it at his own head. His wife started laughing hysterically.

"And just what in the hell are you laughing about?" he demanded. "You're next!"

438

The Grand Dragon of the local Ku Klux Klan bought his wife a porcelain statue of a mouse, but as she unwrapped it, it fell to the floor and broke. Out of the rubble came a real mouse. As it ran around the floor, dozens of other mice came out of the woodwork and joined it. Then they ran out the door and down the street, and more mice joined in from each house they passed. Soon hundreds, then thousands of mice were streaming down Main Street toward the lake, which they all jumped into and drowned.

Excitedly, the man ran back to the store from which he had bought the porcelain mouse and told the owner the story.

"Listen, pal," the store owner said, "we don't make any guarantees on the porcelain statues."

"No, no, that's not why I'm here," said the impatient man. "What I want to know is, how soon can you get me a statue of a nigger?"

439

A man who had given his wife a black eye was hauled into court for assault and battery. The judge listened to his sob story and let him off with probation. The next day the man was back before the same judge, having blackened his wife's other eye.

"Well, Judge, it was this way," he explained to the court. "Yesterday was a difficult day for me—here in court, surrounded by all these lawyers. Judge, my nerves were shot. I thought a little drink might help . . . and another and another. When I finally made it home, the little woman was waiting for me. 'You good-for-nothing drunk,' she said.

"Judge, I didn't do a thing then. I thought about the condition I was in and I could see maybe she had a point. Then she said, 'You lazy, no-good bum.' And Judge, I thought about the way I'd let my job go—and the rent being due—and again I didn't say a word or do a thing because I could see maybe she had a point.

"But, Judge, then she said, 'If that asshole of a judge had any backbone, you'd be behind bars right now.'

"And, Judge—that slur on your character was more than I could bear."

440

The HUSTLER Dictionary defines *fruit and fiber* as: a queer with a panty shield.

441

A man picked up a woman in a bar one night, and they decided to go to her place. Once they arrived, they began to undress. He got naked first and lay in bed watching her. She moved over to a big dresser. She took off her wig, artificial left arm, artificial right leg and over-size fake breasts, plucked out her wooden right eye and pulled out her false teeth. She placed everything neatly on the dresser.

Seeing a look of wonder on the guy's face, she asked, "What's the matter, honey?"

"Nothing, really," the guy replied. "I'm just wondering whether to stay here or get on the dresser."

442

Q: What do you get when you cross an alligator with a
   Doberman pinscher?
A: An all-white neighborhood.

443

The HUSTLER Dictionary defines *WASP* as: someone who thinks Taco Bell is the Mexican phone company.

444

In Africa a missionary was out walking one day when he came face-to-face with a hungry man-eating lion. He sank to his knees and began to pray for his life when suddenly the lion got down on its knees beside him.

"Dear brother lion," the missionary said, "how wonderful it is to see you joining me in prayer when just a moment ago I feared for my life—"

The lion growled at him angrily, "Don't interrupt me while I'm saying grace!"

445

God had just spent six days creating the heavens and the earth, and since it was the seventh day, He rested. He and the Archangel Gabriel sat back admiring His handiwork. "Y'know, Lord," Gabriel said, "You've done one helluva job—excuse my French. Those majestic peaks, the oceans, the sea creatures and all the animals from fleas to elephants—what a superb job! And the heavens! What a touch, that Milky Way!"

God beamed.

"I just have the smallest suggestion, if You'll excuse my presumption," Gabriel continued. "You know those ample humans You put in the Garden of Eden?"

God nodded, a frown furrowing His brow.

"Well," said Gabriel, "I was just wondering whether they shouldn't have a different set of genitals, as do all the other creatures?"

God reflected upon this for a minute; then a smile

crossed His face. "You're right, Gabe!" He exclaimed. "I'll give the dumb one a cunt!"

446

A midget was on trial, accused of using a bucket to rape a six-foot-tall, three-hundred-pound fat woman. In court his lawyer stood him on a bucket and showed how, with one kick, the woman could have knocked over both the bucket and the defendant.

The midget was acquitted, but the judge knew in his heart that the little fellow was guilty. He took him aside and said, "It's all over now, and you can't be tried twice for the same crime, but I know damn well you did it. How?"

The midget winked. "The bucket, Your Honor."

"But didn't your lawyer—? Couldn't the woman have—?"

"I didn't stand on it, silly," said the midget. "I put it over her head and swung from the handle."

447

Q: If Tarzan and Jane were Jewish, what would Cheetah be?

A: A fur coat!

448

The HUSTLER Dictionary defines *ultimate rejection* as: your hand falling asleep while you're beating off.

449

The President was flying back to Washington after visiting Key West. As his helicopter passed over the Florida Everglades, he spotted two white men in a speedboat dragging a Haitian behind them on a rope. The President asked the pilot to bring the chopper down alongside the boat. Once in hearing range, the President turned on the microphone and yelled, "I sure do think it's wonderful of you two boys to take a Haitian water-skiing! It's refreshing to see that you've learned to live together in peace!"

As the helicopter flew off, one of the boaters turned to the other and said, "He may be President, but he don't know jack-shit about huntin' alligator."

450

The HUSTLER Dictionary defines *crying shame* as: when a man goes through one inch of hair, then one inch of pussy and runs out of peter.

451

A couple of miserly old women were trying to sneak into a pay toilet without turning loose of their dimes. Each was going up and down the line peeking under the doors, hoping to find someone who was almost finished and would open up soon.

One old gal come to a stall occupied by a local pervert who would slip into women's toilets and jerk off. After a quick glance she motioned to her friend to look. They stared in amazement for a while, and then one whispered, "Did you see the size of that tampon?"

"Yes," the other old lady hissed, "and the poor thing must be sick. She's squeezing pus out of it!"

452

Q: Did you hear about the new terrorist doll?
A: You wind it up, and it explodes in your hand!

453

Three Marines were sitting in a bar, talking about the most frightening sound they had ever heard in their lives. "I was stuck in a car on a railroad track one time," said the first Marine, "and I heard this train whistle down the track. Talk about scared!"

"I was in Nam," said the second, "and every time I'd hear VC mortar shells coming, I'd just about shit."

"Well," said the third Marine, "I was down in San Diego one time on liberty, and I picked this broad up in a bar. We went back to her room, and just when we were getting it on, this guy busts down the door. 'It's my husband!' she screams. So I climbed out the window, bare-assed naked. But we were six stories up, and I had to inch along a window ledge. Just then the husband stretched out the window and grabbed me by the balls with his right hand."

"What's that got to do with the most frightening sound you ever heard in your life?" asked the first Marine.

"You ever hear a guy try to open a straight razor with his teeth?!"

454

Tragedy struck at the zoo one day when a man fell into the polar bear pit and was eaten alive by one of the animals. A petition was filed to have the bear destroyed as a public menace. When the judge talked to the keeper, he mentioned that the man had been a member of the Moral Majority.

"So that explains it!" the zookeeper said.

"Explains what?" the judge asked.

"Ever since the accident," the zookeeper explained, "the bear's been licking his ass continuously. He must've been trying to kill the taste!"

455

A gay from California was telling his friend about eating hog nuts while in West Virginia. "It damned near killed me," he said.

"How come?" asked his friend.

"Why, that hog almost kicked me to death!"

456

A 90-year-old woman caught her 90-year-old husband in a hotel room in bed with a young girl. Furious, she threw him out the sixth-story window. Later, during police questioning, they asked her why. "It's simple," she replied. "At 90 years old, I figured if he could fuck, he could fly."

457

A Polack came home late one night and, without a word, grabbed his wife and made passionate love to her. The next morning the satisfied woman said, "After three months of marriage, why did it take you so long to finally lay me?"

"Well," he explained, "I didn't know you were putting out until the guys at the bowling alley all told me."

458

A salesman checked into a motel in Texas. The next morning he came down from his room looking rattled.

"Is something wrong?" asked the motel clerk.

"Are you kidding?" the salesman replied. "About three o'clock this morning I woke up with a huge fucking cowboy sitting on my chest. He had a gun in my face, and he told me to blow him or he'd blast my fucking head off."

"What did you do?" asked the clerk.

The salesman answered, "You hear any shooting?"

459

Gus went to see a lawyer about a divorce. The lawyer asked, "What *grounds* do you have?"

Gus answered, "Just the usual. Front yard, backyard and a tiny little strip on each side."

The lawyer elaborated, "No, I meant to ask, 'Do you have a *grudge*?' "

Gus shrugged, "Yeah, we have one—but we keep it so full of junk, we can't get the car in it."

The lawyer sighed, "Let me be more specific. Is your wife a *nagger*?"

Gus grunted, "No, but I caught her screwing one, and that's why I want the divorce."

460

When the betrayed husband caught another man in bed with his wife, he ushered the other fellow at gunpoint out to his garage workshop. There the cuckhold tightly clamped the cheating man's cock in the vise on the workbench, removed the handle from the vise and, with a grin, picked up a hacksaw.

Already scared shitless, the man screamed, "My God, you're not going to saw my cock off, are you?"

The husband handed the man the hacksaw and chuckled, "Nope, you are. I'm gonna set the garage on fire."

461

A biker's wife was seriously ill, and after calling all over town, he finally found a young doctor who would make a house call. Upon arriving, the physician went upstairs to examine the lady. Minutes later he came back down and said, "I need a screwdriver." The biker found one and gave it to the doctor, who raced upstairs. But he was soon back again.

"Got any pliers?" Once more the now-frantic biker

found the requested item and gave it to the doctor, who ran upstairs. Almost immediately he returned. "I need a hammer and a chisel."

"Dammit, Doc!" exclaimed the biker. "What the fuck is wrong with my old lady?"

"I don't know yet," said the doctor. "I can't get my fuckin' bag open."

462

Q: Why did God make pussy smell like fish?
A: Because he made sperm look like tartar sauce.

463

On a foggy night in London a somewhat inebriated Englishman was walking through Trafalgar Square. Suddenly, he heard a voice from up ahead. "Has anyone seen a naked lady?" it asked. The drunk thought that was rather strange, but he proceeded onward. Some moments later a dim form appeared before him— a young Englishwoman walking bare-assed naked through the square! As the girl rushed past, the voice came through the fog again. "Has anyone seen a naked lady?"

"I have!" the drunk shouted back.

"Well, fuck her," the voice replied. "She's paid for!"

464

Joe's wife came in and found him packing his clothes. "And just where do you think you're going?" she demanded.

"I'm going to Australia," he replied. "I read where they are paying men 10 bucks a shot for stud service to lonely women in the outback region."

At once the woman pulled out her own suitcase and started packing.

"And just where do you think you're going?" her husband asked.

"To Australia," she answered. "I've just got to see how you can live on $20 a month."

465

A Jew and a Chinaman were in a bar, talking one night about Pearl Harbor. When the Jew complained about the horrible deed the Chinese had done, the Chinaman protested, "The Japanese attacked Pearl Harbor, not us Chinese!"

"Japanese, Chinese, they're all the same to me," said the Jew.

The Chinese fellow then began talking about the sinking of the *Titanic* and wondered if the Jew felt no responsibility for that tragic act.

"Wait a minute, "the Jew cried out. "The Jews didn't

have anything to do with that! The *Titanic* was sunk by an iceberg!"

The Chinaman muttered, "Iceberg, Goldberg, they're all the same to me."

466

The HUSTLER Dictionary defines *bushwacker* as: a woman who masturbates.

467

Two black Texas prostitutes took a bus to California. En route the bus stopped in a small Arizona town, where two Indian women got on and sat down in the seats in front of the black ladies. Curiosity overwhelmed one of the hookers, and after a while she reached up and tapped one of the Indians on the shoulder. "Is y'all *real* Indians?" she asked.

The woman seemed bewildered, and it very quickly became apparent that she didn't speak any English. Then the woman in the other seat answered for her, "Yes, I'm Arapaho, and my friend is a Navaho."

"Oooh, I can relate to that," the black woman replied happily. "Me, I'm a Dallas ho'! And my friend heah, she's a Fort Worth ho'!"

468

A Polack went to the movies, bought a ticket and walked in to see the film. A minute later he reappeared at the box office and purchased another ticket; then a few minutes after that he came back and asked for yet another.

"What's the problem?" questioned the cashier. "I've already sold you two tickets."

"I know," said the Polack. "But every time I try to get in, the guy at the door takes 'em and tears 'em up."

469

Q: What do you call a child raised in a house of ill repute?

A: A brothel sprout.

470

Saint Peter had just finished interviewing three Polacks who wanted to get into heaven. Since they were borderline cases, he decided that if they could each answer a religious question, he'd let them in.

Turning to the first Polack, Saint Peter asked, "What is the meaning of Easter?"

"That's easy," came the answer. "It's when you dress up in costumes and go trick or treating."

"Sorry," Saint Peter replied. "I am afraid that is wrong. Same question, number 2: What is the meaning of Easter?"

"Simple," said the second Polack. "It's when you buy presents for everybody and sing Christmas songs."

"No," replied Saint Peter, "your answer is also incorrect. Now, how about you, number 3? Can you tell me the meaning of Easter?"

"I think so," came the answer. "It's when Jesus arose from the grave—"

"That's right!" exclaimed Saint Peter. "Do you know anything else about Easter?"

"Yes," answered the third Polack, "if he sees his shadow, we have six more weeks of winter!"

471

Q: What do you call four Mexicans who are stuck in quicksand?

A: *Cuatro sinko.*

472

A man walked into his favorite bar and ordered a round of drinks for the house. After serving everyone, the bartender asked what the occasion was.

"I finally outdid my older brother!" the man exclaimed. "I'm now taller than he is!"

"Aw, come one," the bartender said, "you're a little old to still be growing."

"I'm not growing," snickered the man. "He was in a car wreck, and both his legs got cut off."

473

The HUSTLER Dictionary defines *surrogate mother* as: a womb for rent.

474

The English teacher in a predominantly Hispanic public school decided it was time for the weekly vocabulary lesson. "What's the difference between *select* and *choose*, Ramon?" she asked one bright-eyed Mexican.

"*Select* is when we pick something," he answered, "and *choose* is what we wear on our feet."

475

The day after the senior prom two buddies were discussing how far they had gotten with their dates after the dance.

"You should have been there," gloated Jack. "I made

Joy so hot, she let me get a hotel room. I took off her dress, her bra, and finally her panties hit the floor."

"Go on," urged Rick. "What happened next?"

"Well, I took her out on the balcony so we could do it, but it was so damn cold, I just couldn't keep my dick hard," admitted Jack. "So we dressed and went home."

"What!" exclaimed Rick. "Why in the hell didn't you take her back in the room and fuck her there?"

"You stupid shit," Jack shot back, "didn't your daddy ever tell you that if you come outside, you won't get the girl pregnant?"

476

The HUSTLER Dictionary defines *anal intercourse* as: a stick-in-the-mud.

477

The golf nut arrived home three hours late from his weekly game looking utterly disgusted and completely exhausted. He dragged himself inside the house, flopped into his favorite chair and asked his wife for a strong drink.

"That's the last time I play with George!" he fumed. "The man has absolutely no consideration for his fellow golfers!"

"You seem pretty angry," the wife said. "What did he do?"

"The inconsiderate prick had a heart attack on the fourth hole," exclaimed the golfer, "and for the rest of the day it was hit the ball . . . drag George . . . hit the ball . . . drag George . . . !"

478

A man and his wife loved to compete with each other. Everything was a contest. The husband, though, was getting depressed, because from the day they were first married, the wife won every game they played. The man went to a psychiatrist and told him his problem. He explained that he wouldn't mind losing to his wife once in a while, but he had never once won. So the shrink said, "All we have to do is devise one game where you can't lose." Thinking a moment, he said, "I've got it! Go home and challenge your wife to a pissing contest. Whoever can piss higher on the wall, wins. There's no way you can lose!"

The husband went home, leaped out of the car and yelled at his wife in the backyard, "Honey! Honey! I have a new game!"

"What is it?" she asked.

"We're both going to piss on the wall here," he said confidently, "and whoever makes the highest mark, wins."

"Great," the wife said, "I'll go first!" She lifted her skirt, jacked her leg up and peed on the wall, making a mark about six inches high.

"Okay," he said. "Now it's my turn."

He unzipped his trousers, took himself out, and was just about to piss when his wife said, "Hey, wait a minute. No hands allowed!"

479

Q: What does a Polish girl get on her wedding night that's long and hard?

A: A new last name.

480

Abe hurried into the church and made his way to the confessional. When the little window opened, he told the priest that an incredible knockout with tits the size of soccer balls had come into his store. Coyly bending over in her short skirt, she'd allowed him a glimpse of her long, sleek legs, then she'd come over to the counter and leaned down so he could see every firm inch of her glorious globes.

"So I asked her," Abie went on, " 'What do you want, lady?' Then she reaches down over the counter so her skirt hikes up over that beautiful tushie of hers, and she grabs for my schwanz! Before I can stop her, she's on the other side of the counter, undoing my pants and beggin' me—*beggin' me*, I tell ya!—to give it to her good! So I whip out the old pork sausage and bend her over the counter and screw her till she's poundin' her fists and cryin' her eyes out, it was so good."

The priest finally gets a chance to speak. "Abie? Abie Saperstein, is that you? Don't lie to me, Abie. I know it's you. What are you doing here, Abie? You're Jewish. Why are you telling me this story?"

"You?" Abie cries. "I'm tellin' everyone!"

481

The HUSTLER Dictionary defines *stalemate* as: a menopausal wife.

482

Late one afternoon, a man walked up to a saving and loan branch office and found that it was closed. After several minutes of pounding on the door, the manager finally appeared. "We're closed!" he shouted through the window.

"What the hell do you mean you're closed?" the irate man shouted back. "Your sign says you're open from 9 to 5."

"Those aren't our hours. Those are the odds we'll be open tomorrow."

483

A brute of a fellow died and found himself in front of the Pearly Gates. "Hello, son," Saint Peter said, jangling his keys. "What did you do down on earth?"

"I was a member of the Washington, D.C., SWAT team," he replied.

"Well, I don't think there's any point in your trying to get in here," Saint Peter suggested.

"I'm not trying to get in," the cop retorted. "I'm giving you all five minutes to get out!"

484

"What seems to be the problem?" the doctor asked Mark.

"Doc, please promise me you won't laugh," Mark replied, "because it's about the size of my balls."

The doctor assured him that as a professional medical practitioner, he would never laugh at any patient's problem. He advised Mark to relax, drop his pants and let him take a look.

Reluctantly, Mark stood up and pulled down his pants, exposing the most shriveled pair of raisin-size balls the doctor had ever seen. The doctor couldn't help but laugh so hard that he fell out of his chair.

Mark was so humiliated that he quickly pulled up his pants and cried, "Stop laughing, Doc, I'm ashamed enough as it is!"

When the doctor finally regained his composure, he apologized sincerely, "I'm really very sorry. I know I shouldn't have laughed. Now, tell me, how long have you had this condition?"

"Well," Mark replied, "they've been swelling like this for about a week now."

485

The biker, drawing up his last will and testament, instructed his lawyer, "I wanna leave all my worldly possessions and money to my ol' lady." After pausing a second, he added, "But only on the condition that the whore remarries within a year after I croak."

Puzzled, the attorney asked the man, "Whatever you say, but why the unusual condition?"

The biker grinned and said, "Because, I wanna make sure that *somebody's* sorry I died."

486

Q: How do you make Polish sausage?
A: Use retarded pigs.

487

While sitting in the vet's waiting room with his cat, a man saw a woman walk in with a very handsome golden retriever.

"That's a beautiful animal, and so frisky," he said to her. "He can't be sick. What's he here for, a shot?"

"No, not a shot," she said.

"He's sick? What's wrong with him?"

"He has syphilis."

"Syphilis? How did he get syphilis?"

"Well, he *says* he got it off a tree."

488

It was Clark's first day in the car pool. When the car honked in front of his house, he ran out. Halfway down the walk, he heard a loud "ahem" and the tapping of his wife's foot on the porch. He turned, and there she was, arms folded, scowling at him. He ran back to the steps, spread her bathrobe, bent over and kissed her right on the snatch. Then he ran back down the walk and hopped into the car.

They rode in silence for a few moments until Elliott, the driver, could contain himself no longer. "Clark," he said, "I don't mean to pry, but our curiosity is killing us. Why do you kiss your wife down there?"

Clark answered, "*Whew!* You guys should smell her breath in the morning!"

489

After landing at LAX, the Polish pilot, visibly shaken, said to his copilot, "That was close! Shortest damn runway I ever saw!"

To which the copilot answered, "Sure as hell was! But look at how *wide* the fucking thing is!"

490

"Sorry I'm late," the biker told his boss, "but my ol' lady passed out in the bathroom this morning and fell over the sink."

"Holy shit!" exclaimed his boss. "So what did you do?"

"At first I couldn't really think of what to do," said the biker, "but finally I just started shaving over the bathtub."

491

Mrs. Verciglio reported her shipping magnate husband missing and became a daily visitor at the morgue. One day, as the morgue attendant uncovered the face of a corpse, the woman thought she recognized her spouse, but she wasn't positive.

"Pull the sheet down a bit lower," she requested.

The attendant brought the sheet down to the waist and asked, "Lady, is this your husband?"

"I'm still not certain. Pull the sheet lower."

The attendant pulled the sheet off completely.

"Now, lady, is this guy your husband?"

"No," she answered, "no, he isn't, but *somebody* certainly lost a good man!"

492

Q: What's the difference between a rabid pit bull and a woman on the rag?

A: Lipstick.

493

Jesse, a utility company president, recounted a recent experience. His wife had been out of town when their beautiful European housemaid sleepwalked naked into his bedroom.

"What did you do?"

"What could I do? I love my wife. I turned her around and headed her back to her own bed. What would you have done?"

"I would've done exactly what you did, you lying son of a bitch!"

494

The farmer's 13-year-old son rushed into the house one morning, waving his first-ever hard-on. "Hey, Pa, look at this!" he exclaimed excitedly. "It's all hard, and I can't get it soft again."

"Don't worry, son," said the farmer. "Go 'round to the cow shed and get two big, heaping handfuls of cow shit—that'll soften it up fer sure."

The boy did as he was told and scooped up two steaming handfuls of cow dung. Just then, the shed door opened, and in walked the buxom dairymaid. "What are you going to do with that stuff?" she asked.

"Rub it on here to soften it," said the boy, pointing to his swollen pecker.

"You don't need to do that," she said, pulling her skirt up and opening her legs wide. "Put it in here instead."

So he did . . . both handfuls.

495

Sleazy Suzie was the picture of calm as the doctor confronted her with a barrage of questions after completing her pregnancy test.

"So you honestly mean to tell me," snapped the doctor, "that you have absolutely no idea who the father of your child is?"

"Aw, gimme a break, Doc," retorted Suzie. "If you backed into a buzz saw, would you be able to tell me which tooth was the sharpest?"

496

The HUSTLER Dictionary defines *premature ejaculation* as: when you start squirting while she's still flirting.

497

The old farmer was having a hell of a time getting his prize bull to mount his cows, so he called the local veterinarian for some advice. The vet examined the bull carefully and concluded, "Looks like your bull just can't get it up, but we can fix that easy enough—watch this shit!" With that, the veterinarian reached over to one of the cows and dragged his hand through the cow's pussy, and then he rubbed the same hand on the bull's nose. The bull took a deep whiff, snorted twice, got a terrific hard-on and immediately plowed away on the cow.

That night, the graybeard farmer crawled into the sack with his wife, who was already asleep. By and by, he began to reminisce about the horny days of his youth. Remembering what had happened with his bull earlier, he reached down between his wife's legs, gave her snatch a good rubbing and then rubbed his hand on his nose vigorously.

Sure enough, his pecker started getting hard, so he rubbed his nose again. His tool grew bigger still. Excited, he shook his wife by the shoulder and whispered urgently, "Wake up, woman! Wake up and take a look at this!"

His wife switched on the bedside lamp, took one look at him, and said irritably, "You old fool—you mean to tell me that you woke me up just because you got a bloody nose?"

498

Three women arrived, one right after the other, at the gates of heaven, and were greeted by Saint Peter. "There will be a place for each of you, once you have confessed your sins," he assured them, looking at the first woman.

"I married one man, but I loved another," she confessed, embarrassed. "So I divorced my husband and married the man I loved."

"Show her to the silver gates," Saint Peter instructed, and turned to the second woman.

"I loved one man, married him and lived happily ever after" was her story. Saint Peter directed her to be shown through the golden gates, and then he looked at the third woman.

"I was a dancer in a cabaret," she admitted with a blush, "and I pleased every man who came to see me — satisfied them to the max for the right price."

"Show her to my room," said Saint Peter.

499

Q: What is "XX"?
A: A black man cosigning for a Polack.

500

A man from the city decided to buy himself a pig; so he took a drive in the country until he came to a sign reading PIGS FOR SALE. Turning in to the drive, he parked next to an old farmer standing by a pen full of pigs and explained his mission. Agreeing to a price of a dollar per pound, he picked out his pig, whereupon the old man picked up the pig by the tail with his teeth. "Ayuh, that there pig weighs 69 pounds."

Noting his customer's astonishment, the farmer explained that the ability to weigh pigs in this manner was a family trait passed down through the generations. Skeptical, and not wanting to be taken for a city slicker, the man insisted on a second opinion. So the old farmer called his son over from the barn, and the boy, in the same fashion, pronounced the pig's weight to be 69 pounds.

Convinced, the man pulled out his wallet, but the farmer asked him to go up to the farmhouse and pay his wife, who would give him a receipt. The man was gone for a long time, and when he finally returned, it was without a receipt. "What's the problem, son?" asked the old man.

"I went up there just like you said," recounted the city man, "but your wife was too busy to give me a receipt."

"Too busy doing what?" wondered the farmer, aloud.

"Well, sir, I'm not exactly sure," stammered the man, "but I think she's weighing the milkman."

501

Q: What do football cheerleaders and Iraqi women have in common?

A: They both shower after the fourth periods.

502

A woman was walking her German shepherd in the park one day when a guy came up and said, "Excuse me, but I was wondering about something. Isn't it dangerous to have a mean animal like that around the house?"

"Why, of course not," the woman answered. "Duke is a perfect gentleman. He never snarls, growls or barks. He's sweet to children, polite with strangers, and even loves a little pussy."

"That's interesting," the man said. "You mean he actually lives in the same house as a cat?"

"I never said I owned a cat," the woman said.